1 - 800

17

800 920 4604

1 800 - 253

. 8877

MEDICAIR

Keeping the Faith Without a Religion

ALSO BY ROGER HOUSDEN

Keeping the Faith
Without a Religion

ROGER HOUSDEN

SOUNDS TRUE
BOULDER, COLORADO

Sounds True, Inc.
Boulder, CO 80306

© 2014 by Roger Housden
SOUNDS TRUE is a trademark of Sounds True, Inc.

Published 2014

Cover photo © iko

Cover design by Rachael Murray

Book design by Beth Skelley

Printed in the United States of America

The poem on page 6 by Juan Ramón Jiménez is from *Lorca & Jiménez: Selected Poems* by Robert Bly. Copyright © 1973, 1997 by Robert Bly. Copyright © 1967 by The Sixties Press. Reprinted by permission of Beacon Press, Boston.

The excerpt on pages 40-41 by Maria Housden is from *Hannah's Gift*. Copyright © 2002. Reprinted by permission of the author.

The quotes on page 74 by Susanne West are from her unpublished work. Reprinted by permission of the author.

The poem on page 106 by Hafez, "It Happens All the Time in Heaven," is from the Penguin publication *The Subject Tonight is Love: 60 Wild and Sweet Poems of Hafiz* by Daniel Ladinsky. Copyright ©1996 & 2003 Daniel Ladinsky and reprinted by his permission.

The poem on pages 118–119 by Patrick Houck is from his unpublished work. Reprinted by permission of the author.

Library of Congress Cataloging-in-Publication Data
Housden, Roger.
  Keeping the faith without a religion / Roger Housden.
    pages cm
  Includes bibliographical references.
  ISBN 978-1-62203-092-7
  1. Faith. 2. Spirituality. 3. Religion—Philosophy. I. Title.
  BL626.3.H68 2014
  204—dc23
                                      2013033329

Ebook ISBN: 978-1-62203-165-8

10 9 8 7 6 5 4 3 2 1

Contents

Introduction

The Spirit of Now

Just sixty years ago, Tibetan Buddhism was the most secretive religious tradition in the world. It reserved its initiations exclusively for monastics, who had to prove themselves worthy of higher teachings with decades of intensive practice locked away behind the world's highest mountains. Now you can sign up in any small Western city for a weekend workshop that will offer you those same practices for the price of admission. And you may combine those Tibetan practices with your yoga, with your faith in Christ, with a little Zen, or with some personal combination of everything.

Old traditions have broken down everywhere and especially in the realm of religion. A 2009 *Newsweek* poll found that one-third of respondents said they were spiritual but not religious, up from 24 percent in 2005. In April 2010, the front page of *USA Today* said that 72 percent of Generation Y (those born in the late 1970s through the early 1990s) considered themselves more spiritual than religious.

These numbers are growing every day, as people continue to leave conventional religion in droves. The reasons for the desertions are multiple: sex scandals, power scandals, the inability of traditional religion to come to terms with contemporary culture and its evolving moral values, personal experience being given increasing priority over religious dogma, the development of a spiritual supermarket offering views and practices from all over the world, and both people within religious traditions and people with none swapping notes and making their own selections from the myriad spiritual options now available. Some people choose to stay within their religious tradition, but incorporate the wisdom and practices of other traditions into an understanding of their own.

Meanwhile, the sharing of therapeutic and psychological methods has become a mainstream activity, aided, for better and for worse, by media celebrities like Oprah and the dozens of yoga and meditation shows on television. The result of all of these changes is a spiritual supermarket, and shopping at it is the movement of the times.

You may rail at what you perceive to be the commercialization of religious practices and of personal stories, but it's happening. And while many may trivialize what they learn into yet another easy belief system or the development of a "spiritual ego" that has suddenly seen the light, others are being spurred to ask questions that they may never have addressed on their own. They are drawn to take the journey inside, and for many, that journey is not just a progression toward a healthy ego—invaluable as that is in itself—but also an opening to the transcendent dimensions of human experience.

More than ever in human history, people everywhere are on a rising curve of *individuation,* developing a conscious wish to deepen their relationship with their inner core. Individuation is *not* individualism. The latter is the pursuit of my happiness regardless of yours, and it has been on an upward trajectory ever since the old allegiances of family and tribe began to be chipped away in earnest by the Industrial Revolution. America, the land whose original inhabitants left the old allegiances behind, is the symbol of individualism the world over. Individuation, however, is a maturing authenticity that enables you to feel not separate from, but intimately connected to, others and the collective good. Individuation requires us to ask questions of ourselves rather than be content with easy answers—questions not just about our personal lives, but the larger, existential questions too, about our values, our purpose, our meaning. America is also an engine of individuation.

Those who are on the path of individuation are the most likely members of the "spiritual, not religious" sector of the population. These are the people for whom faith tends to be more central than belief; for whom religion has become a personal spiritual affair instead of an institution whose belief system you sign up for. People like this are not so concerned with what they believe or don't believe; they want to know *how* rather than *what*—how they can connect to a world beyond their own ego, a world of meaning and value that they intuit to be present, and yet are not always in touch with. And they are willing to use whatever works, whatever psychological or spiritual tradition it may come from, to develop what Parker J. Palmer, the Christian writer, calls "habits of the heart" to form that connection.

Another sign of the times is that, while traditional religions are on the wane in the West, atheism is seeing one of its periodic revivals. Its high priests are bestselling writers like Richard Dawkins, Sam Harris, and the late Christopher Hitchens. The physical universe is all there is, they say, and if there are mysteries in its workings that we do not yet understand, science will eventually unlock them with the rational application of the scientific method. Three pounds of gray matter is the source of all wonders. In refuting the supernatural in any shape or form, a rational understanding of the world also necessarily seems to eliminate the question of faith.

Yet in a debate with Hitchens a few years ago, the journalist Chris Hedges made the point that Hitchens fulminated against the irrational without admitting the existence of the nonrational. Faith, Hedges said, does not necessarily need a church, a mosque, or a synagogue. It does not need to be a faith in something or someone. Faith is a nonrational intuition of the truth, goodness, and beauty that are intrinsic to life and that lie alongside the darkness in any human heart. It is a quality of knowing that recognizes the presence of realities we may have no words for, an intuition that can spur us to actions that transcend our drive for personal gain and even survival.

More than a hundred years ago, William James noted,

> [Rationalism] will fail to convince or convert you . . . if your dumb intuitions are opposed to its conclusions. If you have intuitions at all, they come from a deeper level of your nature than the loquacious level that rationalism inhabits. Your whole subconscious life, your impulses, your faiths, your needs, your divinations, have prepared the premises, of which your consciousness now feels the weight of the result; and something in you absolutely *knows* that that result must be truer than any logic-chopping rationalistic talk. ✑

The knowing faith that James refers to is the basis of what I mean by *secular spirituality.* For those who consider themselves spiritual but not religious, secular spirituality is a way of living in the world according to the promptings that they hear in their hearts. For them, this knowing will take precedence over theory or dogma.

Unlike religion and atheism, the faith that lives in the heart transcends our mania for conclusions. Religion is full of definitive answers about the meaning and purpose of life meant to guide you safely from the cradle to the grave. Atheism is equally conclusive in insisting that there is no meaning or purpose to life at all and that what we see is all we get. A nonreligious faith, on the other hand, allows us to live with uncertainty, change, and ultimately, death, not because we believe that a better place awaits us, but because we intuitively sense that there is an intelligence, an inherent rightness, in the way life presents itself moment by moment. We have faith that life has its own Logos beyond all physical appearances—that life is deeper than our minds can ever know.

Secular spirituality steers a path not only between atheism and religion, but also between science and religion. These days, science generates more wonder than religion. Scientific research has endowed humanity with remarkable achievements and given us a quality of life, not to mention life expectancy, that was unimaginable even fifty years ago. It has also taken up the gauntlet of the big questions—Where do we come from? What are we? Where are we going?—that philosophy gave up on long ago. Because every religion has a different creation story, all of them necessarily based on ignorance of what really happened in the past, it has fallen to science to begin to piece together a viable story about the actual origins of the universe. And such a story is indeed emerging.

However, as yet, science is not even close to telling us what a thought is, not to mention what consciousness is, even as it points to the activity that lights up a thought's passage through the brain. Science is able now to tell us a great deal about what we are and an increasing amount about where we come from, but little if anything about *who* we are. For many neuroscientists, consciousness research is becoming the holy grail, the great undiscovered continent.

Religions, on the other hand, affirm the reality of the individual and tell us a great deal about who we are. After all, there would be no point in a religion if there was no one to save or no original spark that was able to become enlightened through the discipline of spiritual practices. Even Buddhism, while it denies the reality of an individual self, affirms that there is something in us that reincarnates from life to life. Depending on which religious story you choose, we are either sinners or the elected children of God, drops in the endless ocean of awareness or souls moving endlessly from one life to another.

Religion is fundamentally human, created by humans for human consumption. And like humanity, it is both a glory and a scandal, inspired and silly, full of compassion and full of cruelty. Just like us. But it is not, as Hitchens and Dawkins and company would have it, the source of all evil. Committed atheists, like their fundamentalist religious counterparts, live in a world of black and white, good and bad, right and wrong. To the mind of Hitchens, anything that was not rational was not only wrong, but also stupid. Evil and idiocy were always out there—in someone else. Yet as long as we continue to project evil out there, onto some other tribe, nation, or belief system, we fail to see that evil is a product—not of any religion or people in particular, but of the human heart. That is where the danger to civilization lies: as close to us as our own jugular vein.

If all religions were banished, evil would still exist, though perhaps by another name. The Hindus, for example, prefer to call it ignorance, by which they mean not the absence of rational knowledge, but the darkness of a mind that is absent the wisdom and insight that is available when we transcend our own self-importance.

And if all religions were banished, the religious sensibility would still exist. With or without either scientific or religious explanations, we can sense that life is an unfathomable mystery. Its beauty and sublimity inspire in us reverence and wonder, and we can intuit that nothing, but nothing, including ourselves and our own little life, is outside of or exempt from an inherently intelligent, perpetual unfolding, in the present moment. We can recognize that despite our loneliness and feelings of separateness, all of us are intimately joined in one great unity of life, seen and unseen, spiritual and material.

A sensibility like this makes us prone to wonder, to pondering questions rather than wanting comforting answers. It makes us prone to beauty, to experiences of being lifted beyond our usual sense of who we are into a larger, more inclusive life, which leads to love. It makes us prone to joy and to feeling sorrow for the tribulations of others and for the suffering inherent in living. All of these feelings and responses to life are inherent in any religious tradition, for they are all expressions of transcendence, and yet they themselves are not dependent on religion. The experience of transcendence is intrinsic to being human.

Sometimes, whether through meditation, a walk in the woods, being in love, contemplating a great work of art, or any number of catalysts, our familiar sense of incompleteness and separateness falls away, and we feel like we're less ourselves than we're a silent awareness, both personal and impersonal at the same time. We can feel ourselves to be part of a life that includes all things, a life both larger and more knowing than ourselves alone. I say "more knowing," because in those moments we feel ourselves to be a filament in the endless web of life and yet joined even to the intelligence of the wheeling stars. We see ourselves as part of a life that is more knowing, yet ever a mystery to our ordinary mind—a mystery with horizons that stretch away the more we gaze into it.

I don't know what this mystery we call life is, but to reduce it either to the observable universe of science on the one hand or to some external religious code of belief on the other would not allow for my own subjective experience, however unreliable it may be, or that of countless others throughout history. An anonymous English writer in the fourteenth century wrote a book about it called *The Cloud of Unknowing.* Rumi and Hafez, the two great Persian poets of Sufism, couched the experience in the language of lover and beloved. So too did Christian writers like Teresa of Avila and John of the Cross, Hindus like Ramakrishna and Tagore, and countless others.

While religions encourage transcendent qualities and perspectives—with their music, their art and architecture, and their practices—you don't have to be religious to experience transcendence, to experience "the Mystery." You just have to be human. If you are human, you can't help but wonder.

And if you are human, you also can't help but experience longing. It is a common intuition, felt in the marrow and not just in the mind, that we live on the edge of a fullness of life that seems all too often to be just out of reach. A lack or sense of incompleteness can often accompany our days, however successful or happy we may appear to be, and it gives rise to a longing for something beyond the known, beyond even words.

We often call that which we long for "love." The flow of longing for love into the experience of loving and being loved, and then back into longing again is, I suggest, the original and naked religious impulse. We don't want to be alone in this world, and love is our most profound experience of belonging. It defeats even death because it lifts us out of ourselves, out of our common experience of who we are, and into a condition of feeling and being part of a larger life. This is why even the atheist poet Philip Larkin can say in his poem "An Arundel Tomb" that it is

our almost instinct, almost true:
what will survive of us is love. ✎

Love and the longing for it are common to human beings everywhere throughout time; and it is this movement from the one to the other and back again that has been concretized and systematized into different belief systems around the world. Love itself, however, is beyond belief of any kind. In *The Varieties of Religious Experience,* William James wrote that "religious love is only man's natural emotion of love directed to a religious object. Religious awe is the same organic thrill which we feel in a forest at twilight; only this time it comes over us at the thought of our supernatural relations."

Tenderness, compassion, gratitude, awe, dread, joy—these feelings too lift us beyond ourselves and our usual preoccupations. They too are reflected back to us in the figures and scenes of religious art, symbols, rituals, and metaphors, and yet they too are beyond belief systems and common to us all.

The poet Rilke urged us to "live the question"—to live the question of life itself, he surely meant—rather than settle for easy answers, to experience the weight of the question and to embrace its substance with the whole of oneself rather than with the rational mind alone. It is the same with the question of love: it asks us to feel deeply our experience of the whole arc of longing and loving—its poignancy, its pleasure and pain—and then the awe, the wonder, the beauty, the deep peace and fulfillment that come when the wave of longing breaks on the shore, and we know we belong in this world and in this life, just as it is, without either dismissing or explaining away any part of the cycle.

Rumi understood how absence and presence, longing and belonging, are all part of the same cycle. Love, for Rumi, was both a personal and a transcendent affair. He loved his teacher, Shams, and he loved the infinite spaces that were opened to him through their relationship. They were one and the same.

Personal love can do this for us. It can open us not only to another person, but also to a love that is so beyond our usual experience that we want to call it divine. And it arrives in our life, it seems, for no reason—a blessing, a gift from beyond, we might say, irreducible to the flashing signals of brain activity. In this sense, love gathers us up beyond ourselves.

This intuition that we are part of a larger life that embraces everything that lives and breathes is not a thought or a concept. Wisdom traditions everywhere have called it the knowledge of the heart—not the emotional heart that we celebrate with red roses, but an organ of perception that unifies the clarity of discernment with the feeling of connection, that provides us with a knowing in which the knower is not separate from the known. This kind of knowing stems from a person's essence, the authenticity they can live from that exists prior to acquired concepts or beliefs. This is why the heart is a universal image for the true center or nature of the individual.

This "knowing heart" is the true center that can intuit a pervasive wisdom in the way that all life works—not the wisdom of some Creator looking on bemusedly at his creation, but a wisdom and intelligence inherent in every unfolding moment and in all creation itself.

This intuitive connection with a transcendent reality, not available to our ordinary eye or mind, is at the center of secular spirituality. To keep faith with life is to experience that everything—everything that comes to us, whatever it is—has its place in the puzzle of our existence; it is to know that whatever happens, it is all happening in the only way it can in the moment, with an intelligence that will never make itself known to the ordinary mind.

This faith, then, implies a basic trust in the way life weaves its pattern. Faith is not rational. It is beyond the usual binary reactions of good and bad, right and wrong; it is an awareness that is not passive or fatalistic, but actively engaged with and yet accepting of life's twists and turns. It may or may not include the sense of a personal God or an afterlife, but whatever form its convictions take, they are the fruit of intuition or interior experience, not of received beliefs.

The terms *faith* and *belief* have been confused for centuries. *Faith* refers to a matter not of the head but the heart. It implies an orientation of trust and love-for-no-reason. Just because. It is, you may say, the fragrance of the heart's knowing. On the other hand, "to believe" in Latin is *opinor, opinari*—"to have an opinion." So *belief* means the mental acceptance of an opinion.

How can spirituality without religion, without beliefs, give expression to faith? And how can we nurture our inherent human connection to the transcendent without a priest, a guru, or the dogma of religion? These are the questions this book responds to. First and foremost, this book urges us to give a deepening attention to our own intelligent heart, along with an informed awareness of the pitfalls we can be prone to. Then it explores how the human experiences we encounter daily can help us to consciously develop the transcendent qualities of our nature.

The numinous is to be found nowhere if not in the ordinary contingencies and situations of everyday life. The chapters that follow explore how doubt, perplexity, difficulty, change, as well as beauty, love, presence, can all be doorways beyond the narrow concerns of self-interest into our greater humanity. They center on ten themes that deepen our faith in the value and meaning of being human.

Religious and also literary traditions everywhere have always used poetry, song, parable, and paradox to give voice to matters of the heart. Jesus dispensed his wisdom in parables, as did the wild Sufi sage Mullah Nasrudin. The Zen tradition gave us the koan, a puzzle impossible for the rational mind to solve. The Psalms of the Old Testament; the songs of the Hindu saints, from Mirabai in the sixteenth century to Ramakrishna in the nineteenth; the poetry to be found all over the world in all time—these are the carriers of our essential humanity. The language of the heart is a universal language, and this is why there are lines of poetry or song at the beginning of each of these chapters, and more in the chapters themselves. They serve as inspirational reminders that you can refer to in moments of need and also for contemplation as a daily or weekly practice.

A secular spirituality brings heaven down to earth, into the life of our everyday. And, like Walt Whitman, Ralph Waldo Emerson, and countless others through history, it encourages everyone to be their own priest. It bows in recognition of the extraordinary mystery that we are living in this very moment, without wrapping it in a neat bow of explanation. In a gesture of wonder and awe, secular spirituality means bowing not to any god or deity, but as W. S. Merwin writes in his poem "For the Anniversary of My Death," "bowing not knowing to what."

Trust the Knowing

৩০

One day you finally knew what
you had to do, and began.
MARY OLIVER, FROM "THE JOURNEY"

Who and what is it that we human beings are? I ask not with an answer ready on my tongue, but out of wonder. The same wonder that must have prompted Nietzche to proclaim that a human being is "a dark and veiled thing; whereas the hare has seven skins, the human being can shed seven times seventy skins and still not be able to say, 'This is really you, this is no longer outer shell.'"

What is Being? This question was the primary preoccupation of the ancient Greeks. Heidegger, "the great master of astonishment," as he was called, thought that Western philosophy was one long detour from that fundamental question. And now here we are, you and I, a book between us, about to stir the fire that so many generations have tended already. We shall raise the question not in the hope or hubris of some final answer, but that we may light that same fire inside ourselves, that we may fall ever more in love with this wild and mysterious business of living. I will use a variety of terms to point toward this ineffable reality: *the Knowing, the Person, the Heart, the Presence.* While each term overlaps with the others, each will also add a dimension to the exploration.

If you take the word *knowing* and roll it around on your tongue, you will register that it sounds like *knowledge,* but that it has a different, subtler taste. In my mouth, the difference brings to mind the distinction between the words *person* and *personality,* and I can't help thinking that these two pairs are intimately related. They may even reach into the heart of our question.

Does the personality not gather information from the world that it lives in and accumulate it into a body of knowledge? Knowledge that it can draw upon as needed with the powers of its reasoning faculty? Knowledge about Shakespeare, perhaps, or the mechanics of an AK-47? Knowledge about celebrities, the subtleties of algebra or algorithms, or the ancient Hindu Vedas or the Bible? Knowledge about anything, exalted or debased, fine or coarse? The personality—our familiar identity—feeds on knowledge. Knowledge enables us to function successfully in a chosen field. It gives us a degree of command in an uncertain world, and in doing so, it adds substance and solidity to our identity. And yet that substance is only ever provisional and will never bear careful scrutiny, however much knowledge we have acquired.

Knowing is different. To begin with, the word *knowing* is a verb and not a noun. It is a dynamic process, not a static something. It is a direct perception unmediated by the thinking mind, and it may express itself as wisdom. Knowing and its fruit, wisdom, signal the presence of who and what you are. Parker J. Palmer, in his book *Let Your Life Speak,* writes, "Everyone has a life that is different from the 'I' of daily consciousness, a life that is trying to live through the 'I' who is its vessel."

You may say that intuition is also a direct perception unmediated by the thinking mind, and that would be true. But intuition emerges from the subconscious mind; the Knowing that we may also call wisdom doesn't come from the mind at all, even though it may make use of the mind.

The psychologist Daniel Kahneman has written an excellent book, *Thinking, Fast and Slow,* to describe our two main ways of knowing the world: intuition and thinking. To explain his case, he makes use of two "fictions" (his term, to remind us not to take his theories literally, something we should remember for our own inquiry) that he calls System One and System Two.

System One works in the background of our awareness all the time. It makes decisions for us that are immediate, intuitive, and usually emotionally based. It makes snap judgments about people when we first meet them. It just *knows* the right turn to take. System One has its reasons, which System Two cannot know, Pascal might have said.

Malcolm Gladwell opens his book *Blink* with a story of some art experts gathered round a classical Greek sculpture of a striding boy. Several of them had a gut intuition that it was a fake, though they were not able to say why. They just knew. And they were right. They knew without knowing how they knew. This is System One thinking. It is a definition of intuition, which is a form of knowledge. But it is not the Knowing. It is not wisdom.

Kahneman quotes Herbert Simon to give some explanation of why and when System One thinking works—which it does much of the time, but by no means always. Simon says that "the situation has provided a cue which gives the expert access to information stored in memory, and the information provides the answer. Intuition is nothing more or less than recognition." Kahneman's conclusion is that if you have had ten thousand hours of training in a predictable, rapid-feedback environment— for example, tournament chess, firefighting, or anesthesiology—then you will blink in recognition and instantly know what to do. In all other cases, you will think—which is to say that in all other cases, you will use System Two, our faculty of logical reasoning. System Two is invaluable. It is one of the gifts that distinguishes us from other animals. It is in charge of our capacity to doubt, to question, to need verifiable and reproducible evidence.

Kahneman's System One and Two thinking concern knowledge, both logical and intuitive. They may even include the kind of foreknowledge that can arrive in dreams. But the source of the Knowing is neither logical nor intuitive knowledge, though it may make use of either. It reaches into the heart of what it means to be human—to be a *person,* rather than a personality.

When I use the word *person,* I am borrowing from the Christian tradition. The Hindus too have used the same term for millennia. But here's where language can fool us. By *person,* I do not mean a *thing,* a fixed entity that can be located as the "real you," hidden somewhere like a mini you, a little Christ or Buddha or Shiva, glowing inside your heart or mind. The word's origins stretch all the way back to the Sanskrit word *purusha.* They point to a *process,* a dimension of being that connects the individual to the universal.

The same is true of the terms *witness* and *higher self:* to our Western minds, especially, these terms can imply something fixed—some substance or concrete object that is our *real* self, standing behind our daily personality, a self that doesn't die and was never born.

But that's not it, not quite. That's the only way the conceptual mind can make sense of terms like this and bring the concept into language—to make it an entity or a *something.* But terms like *person, real self, witness,* even the word *heart,* as we shall see later, can only ever be symbols pointing to a dimension that language can never get its vowels around. That's why the wisdom of what, for convenience's sake, we are calling the Person is communicated more by a felt experience, a presence rather than words.

The Person isn't a truer identity, because it's not an identity or a *something* in the way we normally understand those terms. It's a knowing presence, a dimension of being, a quality of awareness and direct perception. Like a prism, it reveals the colors of the moment while retaining its essential purity. This is why the Buddha kept silent when asked if there was an Atman, a *Self,* the term used in India at the time and still used there today to refer to our essential nature. It's not that the *Self* doesn't exist; it's that it transcends language and the conceptual thinking that always concretizes things. It points to a dimension of being in us—a silent, aware presence—that knows what my familiar self does not know, that sees what I do not always see, and that is undisturbed by the flux of events that happens with the passing of time.

If there is one form of language more than any other that can communicate the ineffable—and this is the ineffable we are pointing to here—it is poetry. Poetry does not communicate facts; it communicates what cannot otherwise be said through image, metaphor, and symbol. These forms of speech come from the imaginal realm, itself the gateway to what cannot be said at all. You *feel* poetry rather than understand it. It conveys a visceral experience, rather than information. We feel the echo of a good poem in our bones, and we "know" what the poem is saying even if we cannot fully explain it.

Poets throughout the ages have given voice to our deeper nature. They may sound as if they are talking about concrete entities and things—the soul as a bird, the first person *I* as the *real Self*. But we must remember that poetry's territory is the imaginal world that speaks in pictures. The pictures point to the moon. Here are some word pictures from Walt Whitman's "Song of Myself" that evoke the distinction between the Person, the Knowing, and the personality, with its knowledge:

> The latest dates, discoveries, inventions, societies,
> authors old and new,
>
> . . .
>
> The real or fancied indifference of some man or woman
> I love,
> The sickness of one of my folks or of myself,
> or ill-doing . . . or loss or lack of money, or depressions
> or exaltations,
>
> . . .
>
> These come to me days and nights and go from me again,
> But they are not the Me myself,
>
> Apart from the pulling and hauling stands what I am,
>
> . . .
>
> . . . curious what will come next,
> Both in and out of the game and watching and
> wondering at it. ๑

The great Spanish poet Juan Ramón Jiménez frames it this way:

> I am not I.
> I am this one
> walking beside me whom I do not see,
> whom at times I manage to visit,
> And whom at other times I forget; ๑

We get it, we sense it, we feel it—this one they are pointing to, the one who, Whitman writes, "is not the Me myself . . . who is curious what will come next"—who is "both in and out of the game and watching and wondering at it." The one whom, Jiménez writes, "at times I manage to visit, / And whom at other times I forget."

This is the Person as distinct from the personality. What you know *about* is of the personality. The Knowing in us is the radiance, the *presence* of the Person that we are—a knowing field rather than a store of knowledge, the curious witness, ungraspable and unfindable. It doesn't know anything in particular. It responds spontaneously to the environment, inner or outer, with a silent, present awareness that may use the knowledge of the personality as a craftsman uses an instrument. But in this case, the instrument of knowledge is used with wisdom. That wisdom *comes through us,* radiates from us, rather than being anything we decide upon or logically work out.

It's significant, then, that the word *person* comes down to us not only from its origins in the Sanskrit, but also via the Latin *per-suona,* meaning "to sound through." Wisdom seems to come from beyond us and sound through us, in the form of words or actions, or simply as a clear and impartial presence. It's not ours, so to speak; there's no sense of ownership. It can't be stored for future use, as knowledge can. It serves the moment at hand and varies according to the need of the moment. It's a moment-by-moment response, authentic to the moment itself. It cannot be self-serving (in the service of the personality's needs and desires) because it comes from beyond the personality and leaves no trace as it passes through us.

You have probably known the passage of wisdom yourself in any number of ways. When we act nobly, with dignity, with grace and generosity; when we make a spontaneous act

self-sacrifice in some way that will benefit the greater whole; when we act to bring about goodness, truth, and beauty in any form; when we convey an atmosphere of effortless peace, clarity, equanimity, and compassion for others—when these qualities arise, we know they do not *belong* to us as such, even as they pass through us. We forget ourselves and our narrow concerns for the moment, even as we seem to speak from some larger self other than the one we normally inhabit and are so familiar with.

Not that we are uninvolved, like some unconscious channel; no, the field of being that I am calling the Person is "both in and out of the game," as Whitman writes. The Person is intrinsically human and not a visitation from some other world. It serves as a conscious bridge between the personal and the transcendent dimensions of our own humanity, a threshold where the individual and the universal become one.

When that dimension awakens in us, in the form of any of the qualities I have mentioned above, we recognize it somehow. We remember it, and we remember that its passage raises us up to the best we can be—not in some outwardly moral sense, but as a natural and spontaneous expression of those qualities that are intrinsic to the Knowing, the Person that we are. Even if we do not always experience ourselves as that, even though most of us need to remember because we so often forget, we can trust the Knowing Presence that we are because all of us at some time or another have known the true taste of it. And in reality, it never comes and never goes.

We remember that it straightens us, gathers us up, makes us whole (re-members us). To re-member ourselves is the purpose of philosophy, Plato says. Re-membering is a theme in the Psalms. Yoga is literally a way of re-membering ourselves. Hindu and Buddhist chants are designed to attune us to the frequency of the purusha, the Knowing that we are. Remembrance—not

of something past, but of that in us which is always and ever present—is integral to all spiritual traditions.

THE HEART'S KNOWING

This knowing field, our true identity, is the heart of our existence. The heart has been the symbol for our deepest humanity the world over. The Heart Sutra is the most revered of all Buddhist texts, and these are its most beloved lines:

> Gone, gone, gone beyond,
> Gone far beyond, the Wisdom is. ❧

Gone beyond—beyond the dualistic version of the world that we ordinarily live in. *Who* we are stands free and silent in the center of the circle, in the heart of hearts.

William Penn, the Quaker who founded Pennsylvania, wrote that "there is something nearer to us than scriptures, to wit, the word in the heart from which all scriptures come." In yogic traditions, the heart is the seat of individual consciousness. In the Japanese language, there are two distinct words to describe the heart: *shinzu* denotes the physical organ, while *kokoro* refers to "the mind in the heart." All these traditions have a common view of the heart as harboring an intelligence that operates independent of the brain yet in communication with it. In Sufism, this intelligence of the heart is known as the Qalb, "the speaking selfhood" or "the eye of the spirit." *The speaking selfhood*: this is who we are at heart.

As always, we are speaking in metaphor, in poetic language, of something that is *real*—more real than anything—but that is not a *something*. *The heart* is perhaps a less loaded term than *Person* or *Self*, less liable to form an image of something solid sitting inside us, since we know we are not talking about the physical organ. Even so, it has gathered confusions around its meaning. *Heart* can mean different things to different people.

What we normally mean by it is the emotional heart—the one that feels personal joy and sorrow, romantic love, and empathy for others. The yogic traditions have practices to allow these affects fully into our experience—to open what they call the heart chakra, the wheel or matrix of emotional energies located in the center of the chest, so that the more personal emotions become refined with an influx of transpersonal energy. Visualizations, devotional music, and ecstatic dance can open the heart chakra in this way. They can fill the heart with boundless love and compassion.

Such experiences of heart opening are profound and even transformational. Yet the wisdom of the heart is subtly different than emotions such as sorrow, love, and compassion, and these emotions do not necessarily lead to it. Jonathan Edwards, the late-eighteenth-century American theologian, was wary of both emotionalism and intellectualism. True religion, he said, was of the heart: "a unitary faculty of love and will, leading to a tenderness of spirit, and symmetry and proportion of character."

Archbishop Anthony of Sourozh, head of the Russian Orthodox Church in England until his death in 2003, was a true mystic. A seminal figure for me in my thirties, when I lived in London, he was a living embodiment of wisdom rather than knowledge. In his book *Lost Christianity,* writer and philosopher Jacob Needleman mentions to the archbishop how the chanting of the choir in the cathedral affected him. Needleman felt acted upon by the music—made good by it, he said. At the same time, though, said Needleman (I am paraphrasing him here), he was struck by the lack of emotion in the singing. Archbishop Anthony looked at him and smiled. "I am glad you noticed that," he said. "We have worked very hard to eliminate any trace of emotion in the liturgy. What we want to convey is a quality of feeling that is prior to personal emotion of any kind."

Archbishop Anthony was referring, I believe, to the more impersonal resonance of the mind in the heart, the Knowing Presence, that is recognized the world over to be our essential humanity. Every tradition knows of this presence and has practices to open the way to it. In the Russian Orthodox Church, one of those practices is chanting. The old Sanskrit chants in India serve the same purpose. Another Christian practice, since the time of the early Desert Fathers, has been the prayer of the heart, which was adopted by the Sufis and remade into their *zikrs,* the recitations of God's name. Theophan the Recluse, a nineteenth-century Russian saint, wrote these beautiful lines on the prayer of the heart, which are quoted in *The Art of Prayer: An Orthodox Anthology:*

> Images, however sacred they may be, retain the attention outside, whereas at the time of prayer the attention must be within—in the heart. The concentration of attention in the heart—this is the starting point of prayer. ❧

The "concentration of attention in the heart" opens the door to our authentic self, the heart of hearts, the person that we are—the one in the shadows of our usual identity. The names whirl and accumulate around the unnameable. Its gift is discernment, prompting us to act in a way that, regardless of the cost to ourselves, somehow serves the greater good.

The heart's prompting, understood in this way, is perhaps one of the greatest spiritual blessings of all. When we act without feeling that we are the one doing the action, there is nothing for the personality to hold onto and to claim for its own. Then it is not even an *experience,* as such, because there is no experiencer around to claim it. Surely those are the cleanest, purest spiritual graces of all. There must be countless souls, unknown to us, who have lived and acted from this, their authentic heart.

And yet sometimes the way to our knowing heart opens mysteriously, of its own accord, without any practices at all, by what some traditions would call the workings of grace. It happened without warning for Eckhart Tolle as he sat on a park bench in London, and there are many so-called nondual teachers in the West who claim to have awoken to their true nature spontaneously.

A man I met in South India, called Nanagaru, had spent much of his life as a farmer in a village in Andhra Pradesh. Some thirty years ago a saint came to him in a dream and kissed him on the cheek. Some time later, he saw an advertisement in the newspaper for a book on spirituality and sent off for it. When he opened it, he found the photo of the same saint who had kissed him. It was Ramana Maharshi, whom he had never heard of before. He made a pilgrimage to Ramana's ashram at Arunachala and returned frequently over the ensuing years, though Ramana had died some years previously. His whole life began to turn on Ramana's teachings, and he began to preach Ramana's message in his neighborhood.

Then, some years later, Nanagaru was in Ramanashram when, in the morning, between sleeping and waking, he felt the subtle physical sensation of his mind, his seat of consciousness, literally falling once and for all into his heart. A profound peace and silence filled his being, and it remains with him to this day. From then on, he felt himself to be living by a force other than his ordinary personality.

Now, do I know that Nanagaru actually experienced what he said he did? I can only say that when he told me this story, it rang true. And within minutes of meeting Nanagaru, as I will relate more fully in a later chapter, I was aware that my own body and mind were pervaded with silence—a silent awareness, a clarity free of thought in which there was a continuous stream of connection with all life. For some days after that encounter I was undivided, without the competing voices of the dualistic world in which we live—both inside our heads and in the external world. This was tangible proof for me: the Knowing that we are manifests as a tangible presence, and that presence can be contagious.

It was a blessed state indeed. While I was with Nanagaru, and for some time afterward, my mind was a lake without a ripple. At the same time there was absolutely nothing exalted about it. It was so clear and simple as to be almost nothing at all; it was a return to our natural ordinariness, you might say. There was nobody special in that clarity, only a deep stillness without any of the ripples caused by the one who is more used to being somebody in a world of somebodies.

In this sense, it was not an experience I was having at all, because my customary sense of self, the one who "has" experiences, had retired from view for the time being. Even so, that same familiar self is always liable to bounce back and claim that or any other experience as its own, as something happens to convince that self that it has some kind of spiritual authority or standing. This may even be happening now as I write this, without my being aware of it, which is why writing or speaking about personal spirituality is always a perilous endeavor.

ON WHOSE AUTHORITY?

Spiritual traditions have always mistrusted—and in the case of Christianity, even feared—the authority of subjective experience. After the early Christianity of the desert evolved into the monastic communities of the Middle Ages, mystical experience was not encouraged or favored. Daily work and the communal liturgy were the rules of the day, and the ecstatic songs and visions of a John of the Cross or a Teresa of Avila were the exceptions and not the rule. This is why most Christian mystics, both past and present, remain relatively unknown to Christians.

If you are building an international organization, you want a generally recognized chain of command and a mission statement that applies to everyone. Personal revelation was suspect because it bypassed dogma and the authority of the clergy. You can't have people voicing personal revelations that might bring down the whole house of cards. This is why so many of the great Christian mystics—Meister Eckhart and John of the Cross, to name but two—were always running the risk of heresy and death at the hands of the Inquisition. As a result, Christianity has found itself sadly lacking in methods and practices of contemplation, and without the formidable and sophisticated spiritual maps of Eastern traditions, whose foundations rest on empirical observation and practice.

And yet the Eastern traditions too have suffered the tension between orthodoxy and personal revelation. Al Hallaj, the great Persian Sufi mystic of the ninth century, was cut into pieces in Baghdad for proclaiming, "I am the Truth," and "There is nothing wrapped in my turban but God." Even when his legs were being sawn off, and then his hands, he kept saying, "I am the Truth," smiling even as they chopped off his head. Al Hallaj went beyond all religious ritual and dogma and looked for God down at the bottom of the well of the heart.

In his book *Confessions of a Buddhist Atheist,* Stephen Batchelor describes the realization that gradually dawned on him after having spent some years in a Tibetan Buddhist monastery in Switzerland:

> I was being indoctrinated. Despite a veneer of open, critical inquiry, Geshe Rabten did not seriously expect his students

to adopt a view of Buddhism that differed in any significant respect from that of Geluk orthodoxy. I realized that to continue my training under his guidance entailed an obligation to toe the party line. This felt like a straitjacket. I could not accept that one view of Buddhism formulated by Tsongkhapa in fourteenth century Tibet could be the definitive interpretation of the Dharma, valid in all places for all time. Moreover, to arrive at conclusions that contradicted orthodoxy was, for Geshe, not only anathema but immoral. To believe there is no rebirth and no law of moral causation is an evil mental act that will lead to confusion and anguish in this life and hellfire in the world to come. And you did not need to say or do anything to commit it. All I had to do was hold an incorrect opinion in the privacy of my own mind. Such "wrong view" is a thought crime, listed in the classical texts alongside murder, robbery, and rape. ❧

The era of absolute truth is over. The aberrations and idiosyncrasies of all traditions become plain when they rub shoulders as intimately as they do today. And anyway, we are now in an era equally fraught with danger, one in which supremacy is given to the authority of personal experience. We value experience so highly that we will do anything to gain it: life experience, sexual experience, mystical experience, peak experience. Our cultural heroes are all addicts of intensity; they are those driven to climb the highest mountains, run the fastest miles, make the quickest million, see the finest gurus, do the most meditation.

Living as we do in a culture of self-made individualism, it's not surprising that we might apply the same standards to our spiritual life that we do to our career. Without even knowing we are doing it, we can go about collecting genuine experiences—a radiant clarity, a devotional upwelling, empowerments from our local lama—to check off on some spiritual curriculum vitae. The Tibetan master Chögyam Trungpa had a name for it: spiritual materialism.

We are prone to it because we all have a personality that depends in part on the approval and validation of others to fill the hole in its middle. Spiritual experiences or authority can often seem to plug the gap. Our personality—pretty much anyone's personality—can sense its own insubstantiality and is liable to try anything to fill itself up.

Spiritual experiences of any kind—visions, visitations, realizations, insights—can open the door to a view on reality we may have never known existed. They are gifts and blessings along the path, and without them—without any hint or sign of some reality beyond our everyday worldview—surely there would be no impetus to wonder how we got here at all. Yet these experiences turn against us when we claim them for our own.

The value of spiritual experiences, whatever form they may take, lies in the degree to which they serve to loosen our familiar sense of identity, rather than prop it up with more self-satisfaction. In an era of personal rather than institutional authority, it becomes our own responsibility, with the support of our spiritual friends, to know that graces of the spirit are not ours to own. People of like mind may be part of a community that has no name, whose members are spread all over the globe, and yet who recognize each other instantly on meeting. Or you may be no more than two or three friends who gather together.

Whatever form your community takes, one of its functions will be to remind you to keep faith with who and what you are. The *Person,* the one whose *authentic heart* acts and speaks—*the speaking selfhood*—this we can trust in each other beyond measure. But how do we know that we are hearing the true voice and not some egoic imitation? I don't know; I've been fooled more than once, like with the three-card trick where the queen is never the card you think it is. I've fooled myself too, imagining I was speaking truth when I was merely speaking cleverly.

But if there's one thing that can ring true when *the Person* is present it is the feel of the air in the room. *The Person* speaks or remains silent, and you feel clarified, more alive, as if an extra burst of oxygen has slipped through a crack in the window. That extra oxygen is a tangible presence; you can taste it on the tongue, feel it in your body, know it in your heart. This is what I felt in the presence of Nanagaru.

THE TANGIBLE PRESENCE

The doorway to *Presence* lies in being present where we are, in the embodied moment we are living now. Teachers in all times and places have spoken of the importance of being attentive to the present moment. But why?

When we gather our attention in this way, bringing it back to the sensations and breath of the body, we can become aware of our passing mood, or our itchy thigh, or our fantasy of this or that. But we become aware too of the stream of our own aliveness, the current that hums along in us all the while, as energy rather than form. The more we give attention to it, the more we feel it as ourselves, the more our idea of ourselves can loosen. Then the seemingly continuous thread of our mind-made identity, fuelled by the past and spinning on already into some imagined future, dissolves when we arrive where we always already are.

A strange thing can happen then. Rather than having a point of view, we may rather become part of the view itself, not separate from anything else. Not that we disappear or become self-effacing; more that we begin to resume a proportionate place in the pattern of things. The quality of feeling that emerges from attentiveness like this is one of spaciousness. There is room, plenty of room, for the arrival and departure and changing of shape of the phenomena passing across the mind. The air is clear and spacious, and yet paradoxically, we seem to carry more weight. If we speak, our words are likely to have more substance.

When we open to this *Presence,* which is indeed tangible, we are expanding from the now to the *Now.* Our bodily presence, wherever we are, is there along with everything else: the cawing crows, the rustling wind, the whirr of the computer fan, the streaks of the afternoon sun through a window blind. Yet this physical world in and around us, which we take so naturally for the present moment, is only the gateway to the deeper Now, which contains everything that ever was and shall be Now. Rilke speaks of this, as the poet he is, in a letter to his Polish translator:

> We, of this earth and this today, are not for a moment
> hedged in by the world of time, nor bound within it: we are
> incessantly flowing over and over to those who preceded us
> and to those who apparently come after us. In that widest
> open world all are. ๑๑

Is it possible, as Rilke says it is, that life exists not as a linear progression through time at all, but as a continuous flow in which all parts of an apparent sequence of events are present in each other all the time? If so, then the various "stages" of our life are present all the time; the generations that precede us and that come after us are present all of the time. If Rilke is correct, then life is a hologram, not a three-dimensional story that ends in death.

This, just this, is the Now that is always and ever timeless, rather than one moment that precedes and is followed by the next around a clock. This, just this, is the Knowing that we are and that everything else is, and from which the world emerges. Yet we can enter it at this moment now of clock time, as soon as we begin to pay attention to our felt experience of the world we are living in—to the warmth in our chest, say, or to the breath brushing over our lips. One simple doorway in the now can open to the Now, to the stream of life that we are in individualized form. This is the Presence, the Knowing Aliveness, that we are in our heart of hearts, that doesn't come and doesn't go.

Could that mean, then, that who we are never goes anywhere, whether we live or die? Better maybe to forego the answers and remember Rilke again. In his *Letters to a Young Poet,* he writes:

> I would like to beg you dear Sir, as well as I can, to have
> patience with everything unresolved in your heart and
> try to love the questions themselves as if they were locked
> rooms or books written in a foreign language. Don't search
> for the answers . . . the point is to live everything. Live the
> questions now. ✍

2

Trust the Mystery

❦

Those who are willing to be vulnerable
move among mysteries.

THEODORE ROETHKE

Who made the world?
Who made the swan and the black bear? ❦

asks Mary Oliver in her poem "The Summer Day." She does
not ask casually. Her question arises from sheer wonder. Her
work is a continuous celebration of amazement, a rarity today
in a conceptual culture like ours, though she is following an
echo that has reverberated for more than two hundred years,
ever since Wordsworth and the Romantics, and later Whitman,
wrote their ecstasies down for posterity.

Who made the world? "The questioning that emerges from
unknowing differs from conventional inquiry," Stephen Batchelor
notes in *Confessions of a Buddhist Atheist,* "in that it has no interest
in finding an answer. Perplexity keeps awareness on its toes." Who

made this hand traveling across the page in the slanting light of an August afternoon? I look and I wonder and I sit back and I gasp as I realize that I do not know what a single thing is. What is this before me that is known as a table? Who is this that sits breathing softly by my side, her legs crossed and her eyes down? It is a wonder we are here at all and a greater wonder still that I can wonder at it. And yet the more I wonder, the closer—the more intimate, inextricably joined—I feel to this throbbing, wild, and passionate world. I wonder, and I come alive as the world comes alive before my eyes.

This brimming perplexity is what the writer Gabriel García Márquez must have felt when he said of his wife, "I know her so well that she is completely and utterly unknown to me." Whenever we slip behind the name of something—anything, anyone—we stand before an open doorway to Mystery, in which there is no longer any solid boundary between you and me, this and that. To look in the mirror with an open and curious gaze is to encounter the same open door. Philosophy, Plato said, is "a bite in the heart," and it begins, said Aristotle, with wonder.

A few generations ago, wonder and awe were natural responses to living in a cosmos felt to be inherently mysterious. In any one moment, a play of forces far beyond anyone's intellectual grasp or control was felt to be active both in the heavens and in the fates of individual men.

Earlier societies gave form and image to their intuition of being part of a larger cosmos, inherently mysterious to them, through their religious rituals and pantheons and through a deep affinity for the earth they lived on. The Chinese would build a road round a mountain rather than over or through it, in order to sustain a harmony with the invisible lines of energy they felt beneath their feet. Buildings and shrines and even whole cities would be placed and oriented according to the same principles.

In *Caught in the Act,* her book on Chinese brush painting, Toinette Lippe shows how this respect for unseen influences and energy is integral to this and other traditional arts of China. She says,

> The secret is just to move the brush and watch what happens as it happens. Observe the energy moving. Holding on to an idea of where you want to go puts a strain on the way in which you move, and the strokes you make while under the influence of this idea come in little lurches. ∽

You could hardly find a modern culture today more different from these old ways than that of China itself. When the European Renaissance began to make man the measure of all things, a shift in direction began—*a paradigm shift,* to use the philosopher Thomas Kuhn's phrase—that accelerated in the Age of Enlightenment and has accelerated exponentially ever since to cover the globe. The shift was away from a regard for the heavens to a fascination with the earth. It was a shift away from dogmatic religious worldviews that encouraged gullibility and superstition, but also a genuine sense of the sacred, and toward an increasing belief in the powers of human reason and a scientific worldview based on observation and repeatable experiments.

The shift has brought us enormous benefits and accelerated the notion of human progress—something that was unthinkable several hundred years ago, when societies were static, and you died in the same circumstances in which you were born. Progress, it would appear, is intensifying in every sphere of human activity and life. We have come all the way from stone axes to endovascular surgery in just a few thousand years. Everything we now take for granted—the Internet, space travel, algorithms, Google Earth, the postmodern novel—is built on a vast store of knowledge that has taken millennia to develop. That knowledge is civilization as we know it.

All those scientific papers, those treatises on the mating habits of fruit flies and the construction of space capsules; all those fine distinctions in philosophy and theological texts; all those essays on anything and everything from ocean currents to the aesthetics of art to the meaning of democracy—the knowledge we're accumulating about ourselves and our world is increasing so rapidly, exponentially even, that we may be forgiven for thinking that we shall soon be as gods walking the earth. Only in the last few years, the discovery of the Higgs boson particle suggests we may have discovered what brings matter into existence. With the sciences of molecular genetics and biotechnology, it is surely only a matter of time before the secret of life itself will be ours.

But our progress has brought unforeseen consequences—some that may threaten even the existence of human culture itself. We have become like an alien species on the earth, and, at least at the political or corporate level, we have scant regard for the planet we live on and no regard at all for the other species we share the place with.

When Leonardo da Vinci placed man in the center of his designs, he could never have suspected the consequences. Human reason was to become the measure of all things. We have taken the old powers of the gods for our own. We have not only chased God out of heaven, but we have also killed off all the spirits of the woods and the rivers, the sea gods and the storm gods, the faeries and elves and the goblins. We have turned the wildness of nature into the *environment*. Our forests and rivers have become *resources*.

Our language has changed to reflect this shift in our relationship to the planet, to each other, and to life itself. Our technological gadgetry has distanced us from the social world as well, so that friends are now collected on Facebook more easily than in the neighborhood. What was once a living cosmos of which we ourselves were an integral part is now considered to be an external world of resources that exists solely for our profit and pleasure. We have objectified the world, placed ourselves above and outside it, so that we can manipulate it with our technology as needed. It exists to serve our own self-interest, and we can act with impunity because there is no higher purpose than our own.

The Selfish Gene is not only the name of a bestselling book by Richard Dawkins, but this gene is also the prevailing meme of the new atheism and of much of science. It is also, in America, one half of the language of popular political parlance. Ayn Rand, herself an antireligious atheist (she called religion a psychological disorder), trumpeted her idea of the morality of rational self-interest in her book *Atlas Shrugged,* which was published in 1957. It now sells four hundred thousand copies a year, far more than it ever sold while Rand was alive. It is the philosophical underpinning of the Tea Party movement in the United States and the 2012 U.S. Republican candidate for vice president, Paul Ryan.

This is where we are today, in the latest era of the Wall Street raiders. If it has always been thus, then our notion of progress seems to be missing something. For all our technological sophistication, there are ways in which we seem to be no more morally or ethically wise than humanity ever was. Yet the neo-Darwinists and the acolytes of Ayn Rand together would brush the moral argument aside. In their view, the unfettered activity of the market will let the fittest survive, while the less agile will gradually be discarded like so much junk DNA. This, they believe, would lead to the progress of society in general.

The gaping hole in the middle of this argument is there in plain view: it assumes we are no more than pieces of animated meat bent solely on our own survival and on that of our species. Yet the laws of the observable universe and of evolution do not apply to the invisible world of being. If you deny the existence of such a world, how do you account for the fact that something is born and eventually dies? What is this extraordinary something that animates a bee or a dragonfly or a human being?

And when it comes to human beings, what is it that makes them sacrifice themselves for each other as much they kill each other? What is it that comes out of their hands onto a canvas or a blank page? What prompts them to ask questions and explore the unknown? What leads them to question even the substance of their own existence—who or what we are, finally? In the face of questions like these, we can only bow down and confess our perplexity, just as our forefathers have done since the beginning of time.

Science itself is founded on our desire to solve the riddles of the observable universe. Science itself was born on a wave of wonder and astonishment, which prompted not comforting beliefs, but questions followed by more questions. The philosopher Karl Popper said that science tries to refute rather than confirm its own theories, so keen is its genuine search for the truth. But surely Thomas Kuhn, the philosopher of science, was closer to the truth when he showed in his book *The Structure of Scientific Revolutions* that, in fact, the last thing scientists seek to do is to refute the theories embedded in their own paradigm. The last thing *anyone* seeks to do is to refute the beliefs embedded in his or her own worldview. As Warren Buffet has said, "What the human being is best at doing is interpreting all new information so that their prior conclusions remain intact."

Confirmation bias is the mother of all cognitive errors, and it operates in all of us. We are all so enclosed in the way we see the world that it takes a major paradigm shift to enable us to see through a different lens. For most Buddhists, it is impossible to imagine that rebirth may not exist. For most cardiac surgeons, it is impossible to imagine that someone may consider alternative treatment to bypass surgery. For scientists, it only stands to reason that methods of research that have a proven track record in investigating the material world should be applied to every sphere of human activity.

From a research point of view, spiritual experiences of unity and the dissolving of personal boundaries can be seen to be the result of a stimulation of the parietal lobe. Under trial conditions, the parietal lobes of meditators light up as they go deeper into absorption. The researcher will equate the experience of the subject to the observable phenomenon in the brain. Yet the observation tells us nothing about the consciousness of the research subject, much less who or what the subject is. Even so, the researcher will equate the experience of the subject to the observable phenomenon in the brain, since the prevailing scientific wisdom asserts that electrochemical processes in the brain lead to consciousness.

Yet Sam Parnia, MD, who heads the Human Consciousness Project's AWARE Study, tells us something different in his book *Erasing Death*. He documents near-death experiences in twenty-five hospitals. His research shows beyond doubt that even though electrochemical processes do not exist after death, consciousness still continues.

A materialist view of the universe is reductionist. It makes every kind of experience subservient to the laws of matter. It applies the tenets of the known to the mystery of why we are here at all. It chases away not only the old gods and spirits and half-heard whispers in the night, but also the mystery of life and being itself. For a materialist, there can be no mystery that will not eventually be made clear in the light of reason and critical intelligence.

Ultimately, what is in danger of being excluded from the cultural conversation is not the old gods, but the quality of imagination that gave birth to them, an imagination that sees and feels humanity to be part of a living, breathing world with an intelligence that we will never fathom, full of presences and qualities that our ancestors gave names to, but that live on as always even as their names have fallen away. William Wordsworth gives voice to this imaginative faculty in this excerpt from his poem "Lines Composed a Few Miles Above Tintern Abbey":

> —And I have felt
> A presence that disturbs me with the joy
> Of elevated thoughts; a sense sublime
> Of something far more deeply interfused,
> Whose dwelling is the light of the setting suns,
> And the round ocean and the living air,
> And the blue sky, and in the mind of man:
> A motion and a spirit, that impels
> All thinking things, all objects of all thought,
> And rolls through all things. ❧

These lines convey an inherently spiritual sensibility, even though Wordsworth was not religious in the conventional sense. Inherent in the quality of imagination that gave rise to them is an overriding sense of the mysteriousness of existence. Its essential unknowability causes us to feel awe and wonder and also a tremor of dread. "It is through the Imagination," wrote Wordsworth, "that the poet realizes his kinship with the eternal. It allows the poet to perceive the essential unity of man, God, and nature. . . . It is but another name for Reason in its most exalted mood."

"Reason in its most exalted mood" is the mind in the heart, the knowing self that knows nothing in particular, but that "impels all thinking things . . . and rolls through all things." The vulnerability and clarity of feelings like these do not fit easily into a knowledge-based, secular society like ours. Mary Oliver's work, which started this chapter, is hardly a common style in a culture in which we don't want to wonder, but instead want to know. Knowledge is power, and we ache to have as much control as we can over our lives and "environment." We like to know where we are going and when we are going to get there. We have a preference for certainty wherever we can find it.

And yet for those with a spiritual sensibility, the unknowable, mysterious, and often invisible forces in life are not only inherent in existence, but they also continue to infuse existence with meaning. Imagine a world in which everything is known and under control. It would be a flatland. There would be no amazement, no wonder, no edge. I believe that just under our skin, we intuit that we know next to nothing about our lives at all—where we came from, who we are, where we are going, and why. To avoid the anxiety this can arouse might just be why we keep ourselves so busy and preoccupied.

The imagination, as Wordsworth understood it, is the gateway to our stored human experience, which is why a grand flight of imagination can have such a lasting echo through the generations. Fantasy, on the other hand, happens when we make stuff up. You can feel the difference. The impact of imagination sends ripples through your being. It prompts you to think and to feel toward verities that are eternal. Fantasy is derivative. It titillates and remains at the level of entertainment. The American novelist Marilynne Robinson says in the 2012 Summer issue of *Brick* magazine, "We have not escaped, nor have we in any sense diminished, the mystery of our existence. We have only rejected any language that would seem to acknowledge it."

It is the imagination that allows us to be susceptible to the unknown, to the mystery of possibility. It is the whetstone of every creative artist. What happens in creative, fresh writing, for example, happens in life. There *is* a direction that life's energy is taking us, but not necessarily the one we think, not even one that we can articulate for ourselves, even as we can feel the pulse of it in our blood. Can we be willing to trust the invisible current that places our feet one in front of the other? I may not know the outcome of my sentences from the start, but I look to see what is on the page, and they lead me to what is coming next. Writing is like life. You need to show up, and then, well, you just never know.

To trust the unknowing is easy to say, but how much more convenient it often is to fall back on what we know or what others know—or say they know. It is far simpler and easier to live by predigested belief and information rather than by faith. Religious beliefs, political beliefs, social beliefs, cultural beliefs—we all have them in one shape or another because we live in a relational world, in which we are formed in part by our culture and early experiences. We all have core beliefs about ourselves and the world—it's a safe place or a dangerous place; I'm a bad or a good person—that were formed so early that they now direct our outlook on life automatically without our conscious participation.

Yet behind those beliefs is the stillness, the Presence that we are, the great mystery of Being. That presence does not reside in our intellect, our will, or our memory. Who we are cannot be pointed to in time or space. We are nowhere to be found. Who we are cannot be known at all. This Knowing Presence can only be inhabited, there where nothing and no one ever is. Thomas Merton wrote:

> There is no where in you a paradise that is no place and there
> You do not enter except without a story.
> To enter there is to become unnameable. ᔆ

By "paradise," he does not mean some state of bliss divorced from the immanent world. He means a place of deepest clarity and stillness, unnameable and therefore unknowable, beyond the reach of language and knowledge. Yet this presence that we are is itself the source of knowing. We ourselves are the Mystery, then. And the deeper we penetrate a mystery, the more mysterious it becomes. Just look and see. Look into the question of who you are, not with ideas or answers, but with a visceral sense of the ever-receding ungraspability of you. "Live the question now," Rilke said.

When we know this as a felt experience, when we inhabit and trust the silence that words may lead to but cannot reach, then we become intimate with ourselves in a way that is not possible when we remain content with our stories and memories of who we like to think we are. Our edges soften. We become a kindness to ourselves and to the world.

The doorway to the Mystery can only ever be exactly where we are, wherever we are. It can never be in our thoughts about how mysterious and unknowable everything is, though those thoughts too have their value. This brings me personally back to the blank page before me now; you might look around and see where it finds you. Way back in the early eighteenth century, long before Eckhart Tolle's *The Power of Now* became a global bestseller, the French Jesuit Jean Pierre de Caussade coined the memorable phrase "the sacrament of the present moment."

Yet what is happening now—the breath, the sensation of sitting in a chair—is only a doorway to that sacrament, which is timeless, beyond, and yet within all the moments of clock time. It is the silent, spacious presence that is the root and ground of all that happens—not some vague or abstract idea of presence, but the felt and lived and breathing reality of our existence out beyond any ideas of it, on the page or in the mind. The Present

Moment is, in reality, timeless and unknowable, as we too are timeless and also unknowable behind our name, here in this present moment. This is the meaning of these beautiful words by De Caussade: "The divine will is a deep abyss of which the present moment is the entrance. If you plunge into this abyss you will find it infinitely more vast than your desires."

The most mysterious thing of all is whatever it is that inhabits this body, who it is that is behind the eyes reading this book. Victoria Sweet captures this wonderfully in her book *God's Hotel*. She is a doctor, and she describes her experience working in the Laguna Honda Hospital in San Francisco, the last almshouse in the United States. In this episode, she speaks of the "return" of Meng Tam, a patient who had been designated DNR ("do not resuscitate").

> We looked at each other, and Hildegard von Bingen's lines about dying came into my mind: "It is as if the soul, the anima, stands with one foot in this world and one in the next, uncertain whether to stay or to go." That was just it. Meng Tam was undecided. He was halfway between life and death. And as I looked into his eyes . . . I saw them become clear and still, like a shallow mountain pool after a rain, and I knew that he had decided to stay. I can't tell you that I nodded, but I knew, and Meng Tam knew that I knew, that he was coming back. ❧

The DNR order did not allow her to defibrilate Meng Tam back into a normal cardiac rhythm, so, with another doctor, she reverted to traditional methods:

> I called Meng Tam's name, and I shook him, and Dr. Mack started to shake his legs. I even slapped his face a few times.

And sure enough, Meng Tam's pulse returned; it became quite steady; and then his eyes opened and stayed open, staring at me. . . .

In my first autopsy I'd been surprised by the difference between the dead body and the live Mr. Baker I'd known. There was something missing—that I missed, and that I'd missed. And now with Meng Tam I'd caught it; seen it go toward death, stop, change its mind, and come back. I'd seen the anima—that which animates the body and mind. ❧

And I ask myself, who made the world?

3

Trust the Dark

Before you know kindness
as the deepest thing inside,
You must know sorrow
as the other deepest thing.
NAOMI SHIHAB NYE, FROM "KINDNESS"

Who made the world? How did this happen, this sliver of moon that hangs in my window, the dark of the sky that allows us to see the stars? The mind trembles and is silenced. Who made the suffering that comes with being human? Who made the darkness that can descend without warning on the human heart, reducing all hope and love to gray ashes? A dark so dark, so painful, that we would do anything for a glimmer of light, a lifeline showing us where to go and what to do next. How did it happen this way, that to live is also to suffer?

Job, the faithful servant of God in the Old Testament, had no answer to that, except to bow to all the misfortunes that befell him: the loss of his possessions, the deaths of his ten children, and the ravages of the boils that afflicted him from head to feet. His health, his wealth, and his family—the foundations for most people's identity—were all brought low for no apparent reason. His friends, adamant that he must have sinned greatly to have merited such ill fortune, represent the common view that people suffer for the evils or injustices they have brought into the world, and that honorable men are protected from misfortune by their good deeds. And yet we have only to look around us to see how flimsy this argument is.

The story of Job has lived on in the collective imagination of the West for so long because of Job's response to his misery. Unlike his friends, he did not question why his fate had turned so dark. He knew he had lived an honorable life and had committed no great sin. He had a profound faith in the way life appeared from moment to moment. Not that he knew there was an underlying reason to whatever happens—he didn't and there isn't—but he recognized that there was an inherent pattern of intelligence at play in every moment even though it was indiscernible to his eyes.

Job's response to his suffering gave us these famous lines: "Naked I came out of my mother's womb, and naked I shall return. The Lord has given and the Lord has taken away, blessed be the name of the Lord" (Job 1:2).

The poet Jack Gilbert borrows these lines to begin his poem "The Lost Hotels of Paris":

> The Lord gives everything and charges
> By taking it back. What a bargain. ❧

Many of us are given everything in life—breath, a beating heart, loved ones, shelter, beauty—and it is still a bargain even though it can be all taken back again along the way and is always, ultimately, taken away in death. It is a bargain not only because of the joys and beauties and loves that life provides on the journey, but also because of how we may be shaped and honed and clarified along the way.

It's not that periods of loss and suffering are "good for us" and should be sought out. That would be another posture or strategy of the ego, or some institutional madness as can still be found in the Catholic Church. No one wants to suffer, even as everyone suffers. No one would choose to go through what Job did. But given that we do all go through periods of loss, depression, and darkness from time to time, how might such passages deepen our faith in life, even as they seem to bring into question the very meaning and purpose of life itself?

The Buddha famously had his own response: All human life is permeated with an abiding dissatisfaction in the way dye seeps into cloth. Liberation from this, he said—the washing out of the cloth—lies in seeing the root causes of suffering. The seeing itself (through meditation) dissolves the false notions that are behind the pain, including the notion of permanence and a solid sense of *I* whose existence is separate from everything else.

Personal darkness, in whatever form it comes, challenges our conventional notion of who we are. If we are convinced that our daily personality is a solid and singular identity, then a descent into darkness, whatever its causes, is likely to be not just traumatic but akin to a dismembering. In Dante's version of Hell in his *The Divine Comedy,* dismembering is what happens to those who cannot raise sufficient awareness to become conscious of their actual condition. When our conventional identity is peeled away by circumstance, there would seem to be nothing left but an endless emptiness, the ground falling away beneath our feet. The more we cling to our conventional images, the emptier and more meaningless life will seem to be.

And yet the peeling away of those same images can also, if we see it this way, open the door to an entirely different experience of oneself, to a realization that is more congruent with the way things actually are. Along the way, not only Buddha but also Job and Dante will seem to have hit the mark. The same deep insight into human darkness has threaded its way through human history everywhere. It's an existential wisdom, known in all cultures. Job encourages us to open our arms and acknowledge the truth of what is happening, that it is beyond our control, and that there is a way in which it is not even personal. We can only embrace the darkness, whatever it is, wherever it takes us, as Job embraced and bowed down to all that befell him. We cannot transcend suffering.

It doesn't work to cling to some notion of a deeper, inviolable self somewhere beneath our skin, where we will always be safe. We can only give up the world we have known and fall into the one that is waiting for us, the one that is already here in whatever form of darkness it may be. To suffer is to taste life, to drink the full draught. "What is so difficult," wrote John Tarrant in his book *The Light Inside the Dark,* "is to keep giving up our sense of the world so that the world can come to us on its own terms, with its vast, pitiless, loving intelligence."

Until recently, my own sense of the world included the idea that I inhabit a vibrant, healthy body. My body image was an integral part of my own positive regard for myself. After all, I had lived into my sixth decade and never had a day's illness to speak of. I had never been in a hospital. Unconsciously, I had constructed a self-image that I imagined would last forever. Then, when I went for a routine check-up, the cardiologist noticed I had a large aneurism in my aorta. It is a life-threatening condition, since the aorta wall can burst at any time without warning. Open-chest surgery would be necessary soon.

Over the next few days, I could feel my idea of myself gradually adapting to take in the news. It took me some time to register the gravity of it, to let the reality seep into my consciousness. I realized how much pride and vanity, as well as gratitude, I had felt for the strength and health of this body that had served me so well. I felt grief at the realization that it was going to change, that it was going to come under the surgeon's knife. I felt vulnerable, suddenly, and very mortal. I knew from the inside now what Naomi Shihab Nye meant in these lines from her poem "The Art of Disappearing":

> Walk around like a leaf,
> Knowing you could tumble at any second. ॐ

But I also felt more deeply part of the human race. When I went to meet the surgeon at my local hospital, he told me he had a waiting list, and it would be a couple of months before I could have my surgery. Every day of the week, people of all ages were undergoing the same operation I needed to have.

Suffering is normal. Physical pain, or even the prospect of it, brings us down to earth. It humbles us and in a good way. *Humility, humus, humor*—they all have the same etymological root. I was not used to pain, and open-chest surgery meant that I would get to know it well. I don't know yet what getting to know it will mean. I do know that the diagnosis and the prospect of pain immediately began to work on me, to soften the edges of my known identity and open me to feeling more deeply the pain of others. It opened me, too, to the preciousness of this life that is moving through me—not its conditions so much as the simple fact of being. But not before I had put the surgery off for a few months, in the hope that the aneurism would not grow any larger and therefore may not need to be operated on at all. That is to say, not before I had tried bargaining with life.

Every one of us will travel through our own shadow lands in one form or another. My ex-wife, Maria Housden, had to cross a valley that I will never know the depths of. Her daughter Hannah died of cancer when she was four years old. In her book *Hannah's Gift,* Maria tells us that three months after her daughter's death, her life felt completely out of control.

By the sound of its engine, I knew the car was coming fast. I stood on the curb, and with a sense of calm detachment, rolled the image around in my mind. Before the unsuspecting speeder could slam on his brakes, I would throw myself in front of him.

The pain of losing her was more than I could bear. I felt as if I were caught in a downward death spiral; there seemed to be no relief from grief. I had expected, having had a year to prepare for Hannah's death, that by now I would have a handle on things. I felt like a failure because instead of feeling better I kept feeling worse and worse.

My rational mind's desperate attempts to convince me that I had a lot of reasons to live kept getting blotted out by my pain. I felt detached from my body and everything else. Despite having two children I loved, despite my bond with Claude [her husband at the time] life seemed empty and meaningless now that Hannah was dead. The same impotence I had felt in trying to prepare for Hannah's death, I now felt in my grief. . . . Stepping back from the curb, I collapsed in a heap on the grass.

All my life, whenever I had been faced with a problem, I had done what I could to control the situation. I had read about it, made lists, and carefully planned my response to it. I had coped by creating a sense of order in the midst of chaos, by finding something good in it. Now

it was as if Hannah's death had dismantled me . . . Since a life without Hannah felt pointless, planning for it or trying to find something good about it seemed obscene. . . .
Curled up in the grass, I let the tears and frustration pour out of me. Then I slowly sat up, wiped my face with the sleeve of my sweater, and took a deep shuddering breath. The cool autumn air crept into my lungs, filling my chest. I was surprised by its bite. I held my breath for a moment and then exhaled. It had been so long since I had felt myself in my body. I loved how good it felt. . . . I inhaled again, this time more slowly, and again. I savored the fullness in my chest as I breathed, amazed to feel life coursing through me.

I realized then that my body was telling me I didn't really want to die. As I continued to breathe, I softened into an awareness that I didn't need to control my life, deny my feelings, or try to get better. I only had to allow myself to be who I was, where I was, in the moment. Life would do the rest. ℘

It is rare that we hit a dark hole and accept it for what it is immediately. My own little story of an aneurism led me through a few of the classical stages of grief and loss before beginning to settle in my mind as a reality. Maria's much darker and tragic story took her a long time to accept, as the excerpt from her book makes clear. Denial is the common first response to news we don't want to hear. The ego tries to retain its stability by pushing away or minimizing what threatens the status quo.

In his poem "The God Abandons Antony," the Greek poet Constantine P. Cavafy warns Mark Antony, lover of Cleopatra and ruler of the Eastern Roman Empire, not to succumb to this temptation. He and Cleopatra are besieged in Alexandria by Octavian, ruler of the Western Roman Empire. The night before the city falls, Mark Antony hears an invisible troupe of musicians and singers passing beneath his window on their way out of the city. He realizes that the god Bacchus, his protector and the god of music, wine, and festivity, is deserting him, and that he, Antony, is destined to lose the city. Cavafy, the narrative voice in the poem, tells him,

> say goodbye to her, the Alexandria that is leaving.
> Above all, don't fool yourself, don't say
> it was a dream, your ears deceived you: ℘

Don't pretend that you did not hear the music, Cavafy urges Mark Antony. Face the music and say goodbye to what you are losing. It can take time to face the music, and sometimes there is no time. So we bargain. We put off the surgery, we make promises, we castigate ourselves, we fill ourselves with regret, we promise to pray and work for charity if only our loved one will recover or return—anything to avoid the darkness that means the annihilation of the life we thought was rightfully ours. And when bargaining doesn't work, when we realize finally that events have spun out of our control, we get angry, as Maria did. We rail at the fates and the unfairness of life. We rail until, like Maria, we exhaust ourselves utterly. Only then, when the ego has lain down its sword and realized that this darkness is not something it will ever be able to fight its way out of, only then, with deep acceptance, does a new dawn begin to break.

This is the story of Dante's *The Divine Comedy,* which remains one of the greatest accounts of the journey of awakening ever written. It begins with these lines:

> Midway on our life's journey, I found myself
> in dark woods, the right road lost. ℘

Like so many of us, Dante was wandering in a state of blindness through his middle years, in near despair at ever finding his true way in life. When he finally surrendered to the reality that he was utterly lost, frightened, and powerless, all alone in a dark wood of his own making, in that moment, he looked up from his preoccupations and caught a glimpse of a mountain pointing to Heaven, with the sun—the light of consciousness—shining on it. In that moment he awakened, not to something new, but to a remembrance of who he was and always had been. He had been in danger of losing all hope and falling into the kind of death that is the loss of all conscious direction. But, like Maria, who "slowly sat up, wiped [her] face with the sleeve of [her] sweater, and took a deep shuddering breath," Dante lifted his eyes and hope flowed back into him. It was then that he saw his guide, Virgil, who was to lead him to the gates of Paradise.

You might wonder why he didn't pray for guidance, for a way out of his suffering. Well, he did, but his prayers were not of the conventional kind. All the way along his journey, Dante was inspired by the inner image of Beatrice, the personification of divine love for him, who calls him ever onward out of himself. His unceasing prayer was the wish to be by her side. Yet his prayer was not in the form of a man kneeling with clasped hands, but in the form of a concentrated and wordless desire. What Dante shows us is that we are all constantly sending out prayers via the unconscious into the environment. His prayerful state was at its height when he surrendered to the truth of his condition—that is, the moment when he glimpsed the light on the mountain. If we rarely recognize the answers to our hidden prayers, it is because we rarely know what prayers we are praying.

As Virgil guides him through Hell, Dante finds that the greatest virtue is honesty, the willingness to see oneself as one is. A recurring theme throughout *The Divine Comedy* is "Look, look well."—

look ever more deeply with the inner eye. A man has the power to unmask delusion through his clear thinking as long as his eyes are fixed on the truth of *feeling*. It is a felt-intelligence that Dante learned to trust on his journey. He would not let any intense emotion remain unexamined, be it an undefined ecstasy or a torment. He always needed the accompaniment of an effort of the mind—the application of a feeling intellect. Dante, after all, stood on the cusp of the Middle Ages and the Renaissance, between the world of faith and the world of reason, and he embraced both within his own being. For Dante, the ultimate goal of Heaven was not a bodiless spirituality, a vague emotional ecstasy, or a dissolution into nothingness. It was the embrace of everything. The Heaven of *The Divine Comedy* is, literally, everything that is.

When Dante had seen and acknowledged his own darkness, he then did three things. He looked at his fear, he rested awhile, and then he tried to climb the mountain by the shortest route. He was turned back by a leopard, a lion, and a wolf, symbols for pleasure, pride, and greed. He discovered that the heroic stance of the ego, who imagines that Heaven can be taken by storm, needs to be replaced by three virtues that are essential to lead him safely through Hell, then Purgatory, to Paradise.

These virtues are faith, hope, and love, and with them Dante emerged from Hell into starlight. The darkness that surrounded him had been transformed by his attitude of acceptance and humility. He had journeyed from a blind, murky consciousness to the shining dark. He saw that as long as he sought to escape from his "hells" and to shake himself free of pain, he stayed bound. He emerged only by accepting another form of suffering, that of Purgatory. The pain of Purgatory is the pain of self-knowledge—a purgative, cleansing suffering consciously adopted, as opposed to the useless, unconscious suffering of stewing in one's own moods, anxieties, and depressions.

In 1913, in the middle of World War I, another great explorer of the underworld, Carl Jung, went through a descent that has been variously described as a creative illness, a bout with insanity, and a midlife breakdown. He was haunted by visions and inner voices, and worried at times that he was in the grip of schizophrenia or was undergoing a psychosis. But in the spirit of Dante, Jung gave himself over to his experience and worked his way through it with only the light of his own awareness to guide him. That light allowed him to meticulously document the experience in notebooks, which were later compiled into what is now known as *The Red Book,* a huge volume that also includes the many artworks he did at the time to capture his visions and dreams. *The Red Book* is a visual masterpiece, written in elegant calligraphy and including paintings of mythological figures, symbolic graphics, and colorful mandalas.

In it, Jung writes,

> You open the gates of the soul to let the dark flood of chaos flow into your order and meaning. If you marry the ordered to the chaos you produce the divine child, the supreme meaning beyond meaning and meaninglessness . . .
>
> You dread the depths; it should horrify you, since the way of what is to come leads through it. You must endure the temptation of fear and doubt, and at the same time acknowledge to the bone that your fear is justified and your doubt is reasonable. How otherwise could it be a true temptation and a true overcoming? ℘

A couple of weeks after the diagnosis of my aneurism, I had another CT scan, and the next day the doctor called to say there were some nodules on the lung that could be cancer. He had ordered a PET scan, and the first available appointment was a couple of weeks later. For two weeks, my mind went back and forth between the certainty that I did not have cancer and the suspicion that I did. Often, I rested beyond both positions in a calm that held the two poles without being swayed by either. In that peace, I knew with a knowing that was larger than my stories that all was already well, whatever happened. Even so, it goes without saying that I was deeply relieved when the doctor called to say the scan was negative. I could feel the air pouring back into my body and the sheer preciousness of the life I was being allowed to live.

But along the way, that waiting period of two weeks returned me more than usual to my proportionate place in the scheme of things. I realized that I had to wait two weeks because all day, every day, there were people like me who were lining up to have the same PET scan. All day, every day, people were being told they had cancer or some other life-threatening disease. It is a daily and ordinary occurrence that people somewhere are having their lives broken open by shattering news. And I was no exception, I realized. I had no special pass. Yet I could see how at times I acted like I did, how entitled I could be, given the opportunity. I am in line for whatever comes down, just like everyone else. And I could feel from the inside out that it was not personal. It's just what it's like, when you're human.

In submitting themselves to the pain of self-knowledge, both Dante and Jung gradually come to experience a "heart in grace," as Dante calls it—which is to say in contact with the Self, the *Person,* as we called it earlier. This, I believe, is related to what Jung means when he speaks of "the divine child, the supreme meaning beyond meaning and meaninglessness." In being willing to walk through the valley of the shadow of death with his feeling-intelligence intact enough to write it all down in his notebooks, Jung married "the ordered to the chaos," the light with the dark, and entered the realm beyond opposites, beyond even life and death. To find the way out and up, both Dante and Jung discovered, you must first fall down, deep down into the night of your own soul.

For the educator Parker J. Palmer, it was the darkness of depression that compelled him to find the "river of life hidden beneath the ice," as he puts it in his book *Let Your Life Speak*. Unlike Jung, Palmer was unable to write about his depression for a very long time. It was only when he was invited to write a piece on the theme of the wounded healer, in memory of his mentor and friend, the theologian Henri Nouwen, that he felt obliged to put words to his own deepest wound:

> Depression demands that we reject simplistic answers, both
> "religious" and "scientific," and learn to embrace mystery,
> something our culture resists. Mystery surrounds every deep
> experience of the human heart: the deeper we go into the
> heart's darkness or its light, the closer we get to the ultimate
> mystery of God. But our culture wants to turn mysteries
> into puzzles to be explained. . . . Yet mysteries never yield
> to solutions or fixes—and when we pretend they do, life
> becomes not only more banal but also more hopeless . . . .
>
> Embracing the mystery of depression does not mean
> passivity or resignation. It means moving into a field of
> forces that seems alien but is in fact one's deepest self. It
> means waiting, watching, listening, suffering, and gathering
> whatever self-knowledge one can—and then making choices
> based on that knowledge, no matter how difficult. . . .
> The knowledge I am talking about is not intellectual and
> analytical but integrative and of the heart, and the choices
> that lead to wholeness are not pragmatic and calculated,
> intended to achieve some goal, but simply and profoundly
> expressive of personal truth. ❧

Yes, our darkness, in whatever form it comes, is as much a mystery as our light. And for some of us, like Dante, Carl Jung, Parker J. Palmer, Maria Housden, and so many others, it is an even deeper mystery that the light was found in the darkness. Palmer happens to be a Christian, but the dark night does not need a religious explanation, or any explanation at all to justify its existence. It is woven into the web of life, and this is why, in spite of everything—the pain, the tribulation—the darkness can be trusted. It can be trusted not to deliver a particular result, but to have its rightful seat at the table of life, because it is inherent in living. To question its value would be to question the value of existence itself. If we can fully enter it, submit ourselves to it without resistance, even as we cry out in our sorrow, if we can be aware of our suffering as we suffer, then who knows, we may emerge wiser, more tender, and more human. Nothing in life is guaranteed, except death. But enough brave souls have gone before us to suggest that, as Wallace Stevens says, "In a dark time, the eyes begin to see."

4

Trust the Joy

❧

We must risk delight.

JACK GILBERT,

FROM "A BRIEF FOR THE DEFENSE"

The anonymous author of the following quote turns the traditional image of spirituality on its head: "God and the angels will hold you accountable for all the joys you were allowed in life that you denied yourself."

Instead of the solemn face of the saint or the figure of a renunciate lost in contemplation, he gives us the image of joy as the gateway to heaven. The experience of joy in this world is an indication that our spirit is shining brightly. Joy is an expression of our deepest nature, beyond all notions of right and wrong, beyond all dogma and belief, beyond any religious framework, even as it may manifest in the rituals of any religion. Joy is a pure expression of the human spirit. It often appears unbridled, unfettered, and ultimately, for no reason. Joy cares nothing for the limitations and conventions that form the structure of our social self. It can leap out of us not only in some recognizably spiritual context, but also at the sight of a leaf turning in the wind, in a moment of solitude, at the thought of a beloved friend, on hearing the call of the swallow, or just because. It needs no form, religious or otherwise, to set it free. It is a spontaneous expression of our spiritual nature.

Why then would we ever want to deny our own happiness? And yet we sometimes do. Think of the child—yourself, perhaps, long ago—who, full of glee at some new discovery, is told to be quiet by a parent. Or worse, the child who's told she is being foolish in making so much noise about something so trifling. We learn all too easily that if we raise our voice above the crowd, we open ourselves to ridicule, criticism, and the evil eye of plain old envy. That can be enough to silence us for years—for a lifetime, even. We doubt ourselves; we doubt our own voice, our inspirations, the joy of our creative urges—all for the sake of keeping the peace and preserving the mediocrity of the social norm.

A few years ago I published an anthology of poems called *Dancing with Joy* to encourage us to do just that. Because we owe it to ourselves to make room for joy in our lives. In the introduction, I ask if it could be that we live in such a dark and difficult world that it can seem a betrayal or denial of the misfortunes of others, as well as our collective darkness, to jump for joy? Could it be that in embracing happiness we somehow turn our back on the suffering of others—and indeed, on our own suffering—and so deservedly bring down upon ourselves the retributions of guilt?

"Conventional wisdom tells us that nobody goes to heaven for having a good time," I wrote in the introduction to *Dancing with Joy.* "We genuinely think pain is virtuous, which is not surprising given that so many of us worship a crucified Savior."

Today there are many voices that contest this traditional Christian view of the value of pain, but it takes time to change two millennia of cultural conditioning. One of those voices can be found in the penetrating poetry of Jack Gilbert. He offers a very different and profoundly eloquent perspective to the cultural norm. In his poem "A Brief for the Defense," he speaks of the suffering of people around the world, but says:

> If we deny our happiness, resist our satisfaction,
> we lessen the importance of their deprivation.
> . . .
> We must have
> the stubbornness to accept our gladness in the ruthless
> furnace of this world. ❧

The title of his poem states clearly that joy needs defending. Joy can seem up for trial without a defense in times like ours, when the world's miseries and injustices are clamoring for our attention, right here, now, on our screens all hours and days of the night.

But does it help someone else's pain to inflict pain upon ourselves? To keep our own heads down, to not live as joyously as we have it in ourselves to do, is not compassion. Compassion is the expression of an awakened heart. But when we blunt our joy, we dull our hearts; we close them to the flood of life. This is why Jack Gilbert says that to close ourselves to joy diminishes the importance of the suffering of others—because we are also closing ourselves off from everyone else.

Should we not delight in a meal eaten with friends in the warm evening air or in the sight of the sun slipping into the ocean? Does the weight of the world's suffering mean that we don't marvel at our lover's eyes or at the sound of the wind in the trees, or that we push down a sudden and inexplicable rising of joy that erupts out of nowhere with no reason right there in the supermarket, or at the gas pump, or while we're cleaning the floor?

Of course not. These are all normal and genuine expressions of our innate nature. Gilbert reminds us, in a poem suffused with human dignity, that the world will always contain the full spectrum of human experience, and that how we respond to suffering and darkness makes all the difference. He urges us to respond, in spite of everything, with an affirmation of life, which is joy. It's a risk. But take that risk, he urges. Be willing to stand out, to be different, to fully abandon yourself to the life that is rising inside you, no matter what anyone else around you might say.

There may be a further reason that joy does not always get its full place at the table of our lives. Pain and suffering easily draw attention and energy to themselves. Our survival mechanisms instinctively draw us to preoccupy ourselves with bad news, our own or someone else's, rather than with stories of hope, goodness, and joy, which pose no threat. The classic redemption story works not so much because of the happy ending, but because of the trials and difficulties the protagonist has had to overcome to get there. That's why the headlines are always about conflict, killings, strife, and tragedy. No one is much interested in reading about the good stuff. If they were, the media would make sure we knew about it.

Ever since the Renaissance, when artists in general were afforded a special status that in some ways excused them from the conventional rules and etiquette of society, the dark angel has always been thought to be an asset to their work—even a necessity. This is why their eccentric behavior would often be tolerated, even glorified, and the usual rules bent in their favor. Still today, the "bad boy" image of the artist retains its allure. In the twentieth century, it was boosted by the likes of Ernest Hemingway, Dylan Thomas, and James Dean. As the century ended and a new one began, it became Christopher Hitchens on the literary end of the spectrum and, on the other, Puff Daddy with his Bad Boy Entertainment, complete with shootouts; and more recently, individuals like the English actor and comedian Russell Brand, who frequently dismayed the BBC with his antics before they parted ways in 2008.

Yet there are countless poets and writers and artists who give the lie to this old Romantic trope. You do not have to be rebellious, dysfunctional, or even merely eccentric to make great art. Consider the work of Matisse, Renoir, Monet, and Bonnard—all of them painters of light and irrepressible joy. Consider the ninety-nine poems of joy from ninety-nine different poets in the anthology I mention before. Not just artists, but all of us know, in our own way, moments of irrepressible joy, quiet joy, rippling joy, ecstatic joy—pure joy that frees us for a time from our habitual self, with its narrow confines of worries, responsibilities, and self-concerns. In a moment or two of joy we forget ourselves. Joy is wholehearted. It fills every cell of our body and mind with an elation that is a pure influx of Being, of the Self that we are and always have been. In a moment of joy you are no longer a kingdom divided—between right and wrong, this way or that way, should or shouldn't. Joy is substantial, even if it is sometimes as light as air.

Joy is what we are here for, if only we can be trusting enough to give it the room it deserves in our lives. Of course we feel joy when something occurs that we have longed for, worked for, or aspired to. Of course we feel joy when love swoops down and claims us for its own. Love and joy are intimately connected; and yet like love, joy in its most essential form comes for no reason.

Joy, like love, doesn't come on command. A wholehearted love is one without conditions: no dowry, no big bank account, no promising job, no plastic surgery necessary. Joy, like love, seizes us for its own, regardless of our life conditions, and like love, it fills us with an elation, a sense of life and meaning beyond and larger than our ordinary lives. Joy unites us to the full flood of life and to the deepest reaches of who we are.

It has no reason or purpose beyond itself, no function in our strategic world. With no function, joy has no intrinsic use. "Joy is intrinsically useless! It won't *get* us anywhere!" I noted in *Dancing with Joy*. "Joy exists solely in the present moment and never has any plans for the future. When we are joyful, our plans and schemes and intentions all fly out of the window. When we are joyful, we have no future as such, because we are fully here in the present experience." *Our present experience, then, whatever shape it may come in, is our doorway to joy.* Can we breathe it in, open our gates wide to it, allow it to enter our every pore? After all, any thoughts or reflections we may have about joy only happen afterwards, when the experience itself has come and gone. Neither can you repeat the experience, for joy comes and goes unbidden.

"To praise is the whole thing," the poet Rilke said. To praise—to feel gratitude for what we have, and for what comes across our path, rather than longing for what we don't have—is to make ourselves prone to joy. Ultimately, our joy, silent or sung or spoken, is our full-blooded praise and celebration of this life we are living now in this very moment. Our praising joy is no less than a spontaneous upwelling of the Presence that we are.

5

Trust the Changes

One moment your life is a stone in you,
and the next, a star.

RAINER MARIA RILKE, FROM "SUNSET"

My memory is not what it was. My face is not what it was. My partner tells me I snore now, which I never used to do, but I don't believe her. I am changing before my eyes. I didn't used to look like this, but then they don't make mirrors like they did. Fall has come early this year; I was just getting around to enjoying summer. Before we know it, winter will be rattling the windows. I'm in a relationship again. I rather liked the bachelor life, but this suits me better. My earlier marriages have gone the way of all things. I am going the way of all things. Three years ago, I had money. Now I have no money. This morning I was peaceful, at lunch I was impatient, this afternoon I was joyful, and later I was irritated. And tomorrow will not be a repeat of today, nor will next year be like this one. We are walking all of us into the glorious unknown of the rest of our lives. Only two things are certain: it will keep changing, and sooner or later, it will end.

The Latin writer Ovid wrote a book, *Metamorphoses,* in which all the characters are forever changing shape, becoming an animal even, or a flower or a branch of foliage. There is reason in his seeming magic. After all, isn't it true that you never know who is going to turn up for dinner—a deer, a fox, a puppy, a snake, a gorilla? You never know what side of the bed people got out of this morning. Ovid's book was a profound influence on Shakespeare; it was the Bard's favorite classical work. Unexpected change, both inner and outer, runs through all of Shakespeare's plays, and many of his own characters shape-shift as a matter of course. Bottom turns into an ass in *A Midsummer Night's Dream;* Hamlet's Ophelia drowns and becomes a nymph; Hermione in *The Winter's Tale* is restored to life after being frozen into a statue for sixteen years.

Rilke too read Ovid's book, and the themes of change and transformation are uppermost in his masterpiece, the *Sonnets to Orpheus.* In the very first lines of Book II, Sonnet XII, he urges us, "Want the change. Be inspired by the flame where everything shines as it disappears." Join in with the change that is already happening, he says. Want—align yourself—with what is evidently already so. Change happens in every moment—not just in the events of our lives, but also in the cells in our bodies, in our thoughts streaming by, in our moods shifting with the tides, even in our sense of who we are and where we are going. Sometimes we ache for change and sometimes we dread it. We harbor notions of what is good for us and what is not, and we try to organize and strategize accordingly. We like to be in control.

We need to know who we are and where we are going. We like to have structures in place—a family, an income, a job, a place in society—that tell us who we are and give us a sense of worth and meaning. This is hardly a neurotic need for stability and control over our environment—it's a normally adjusted way of being in the world. But if the ego, healthy or otherwise, is the only avenue through which we experience life, then we will cling to our familiar structures by our fingernails when they are threatened, as they will be, by change. We will desperately want to steer our ship in the direction we want it to go. When the ego won't let go of what it knows, it becomes hard and brittle. There is no space for any larger view. A brittle ego cannot bow to a larger truth. It cannot pray, with the Breton fisherman, "Lord, your ocean is so large, my boat is so small."

Our opinions, our beliefs, our security and control needs—in short, our ego—this is what Rilke is pointing to in the same sonnet when he writes,

> What turns hard becomes rigid
> And is easily shattered. ৯

No one wants his or her life upended. No one is free from fear. Even Christ, when he realized that his destiny was leading him irrevocably to a crucifixion, said, "Father, let this cup pass from me. Nevertheless, not my will, but thine be done" (Luke 22:42).

Life has scant regard for our control needs. The show goes on, like it or not. Rilke urges us to join what is already happening; to align ourselves with the fact of change, to flow with it rather than struggle upstream to try to keep things the way they are or to make happen what doesn't want to happen. He doesn't mean for you to be a wet rag. You and I are immersed in life; we have a say in it. We have agency, just not all the agency we might like.

The ancient Chinese had a saying for what Rilke is trying to tell us: "Ride the horse in the direction it is going." It was an attitude that encouraged cooperation with life, with its variables and unknown quantities, rather than trying to control the outcome in advance. It didn't mean you merely drifted through life like a leaf in the wind—you were still riding the horse, after all—but it implied that your intention is best served by an open, attentive mind, one that is inclusive of the larger forces of life around it, whatever they may be. It also implied that you were in touch with the knowing beyond ordinary knowing—"the touch of spirit on the body," Rumi called it; everyone has their own name for what cannot be named.

It is precisely because he has not known "the touch of spirit on the body" that Shakespeare's Hamlet anguishes over

> Whether 'tis nobler in the mind to suffer
> The slings and arrows of outrageous fortune
> Or to take arms against a sea of troubles,
> And by opposing, end them? ❧

He is the first archetype of the modern man, alienated from himself and the world with no apparent access to insight any deeper than the rational or the instinctual self. He can see only two alternatives, and he is ambivalent. He is caught on the horns of a dilemma that neither the rational nor the instinctive modes of intelligence will be able to solve. Hamlet is a perfect character study for Kahneman's System One and Two thinking, which we discussed in chapter 1. Faced with a fork in the road, his mind wants him to go one way, his emotions another. Many popular books on change and business (like the bestseller *Switch,* by Chip Heath and Dan Heath, for example) build on Kahneman's research to affirm that the way to navigate change is to have your reason ride the elephant of your gut feelings and use the elephant's energy to get where you need to go.

That advice can doubtless be useful in the daily affairs of ordinary life. But when you are faced with existential concerns, a subtler perspective is needed. Instead of trying to *navigate* change, something deeper than all your strategies calls you to *be* the change. The horse that the Chinese proverb tells us to ride is neither the rational nor the instinctual mind. It is the Tao: the way things are in their deeper truth.

It is the third way that can reconcile the tensions of the opposites. To trust the changes does not mean that we trust them to turn out the way we would like. It means that we can absolutely trust that changes will happen, and that they're not personal. That's simply what life does: it changes—often in small ways, sometimes as dramatically as a ride on a roller coaster. If we have the requisite bandwidth of awareness, we can also trust that what comes and goes does not define the essence of who we are. The true value of change is precisely that it can loosen our grip on the way we want things to be and open us to the Knowing that is beyond all change.

So how do we acquire the necessary bandwidth?

"Pour yourself like a fountain," Rilke writes in Sonnet XII. To pour yourself like a fountain, to ride the horse in the direction it is going, is to choose to willingly cooperate with what is already so. When we struggle against the way things are, we suffer. When the Knowing emerges in us that comes from beyond our binary reflex, beyond opposites altogether, and when we have the courage to follow that knowing, regardless of where it will take us, we are riding the horse, out of the reach of either hope or fear. We are in the Tao, and then everything, no matter what it is, becomes part of the adventure.

In another translation of Rilke's first line, M. D. Herter Norton renders it as "Will the transformation," rather than "Want the change." This wording suggests not just a change from one set of circumstances to another, but *transformation:* a metamorphosis involving a different order, a different quality of being and seeing altogether. It's not a horizontal shift from one room in the mind to another, but a vertical ascent into a quality beyond qualities—beyond any fixed attitude at all. A fountain has no fixed point. You can never put your hand in the same flow twice.

With Norton's translation, Rilke is urging us to see and accept the changes we face as an opportunity to shift our identity, our sense of who we are, from the flux of thoughts and events that make up our life to the spacious, knowing quiet that contains everything. In challenging the status quo, the change, whatever it is, offers us a gateway to that larger dimension of who we are.

Instead of clinging to what you know, Rilke says, fall headlong into whatever it is that faces you. You may discover you can fly. If you are in the middle of a divorce, let it be that. If you have lost your job, let it be that, and if you are dying, may it be so. Of course, it's not easy. Nobody willingly allows him- or herself to be dismembered, torn apart, crushed like a grape between fingers. The ego will never assent to self-sacrifice.

But it's not difficult, either, because it's not a matter of effort. The impulse must come from something else in us other than the personal will—another organ of awareness, you might say. It's the part of us that knows somehow that, however much it hurts, however much we may be on the rack—however much we may be a sacrificial lamb, it may seem to us—what is happening is true, necessary, inevitable, and ultimately, as it needs to be. "Transience plunges us into deep being," Rilke wrote in one of his letters.

I encountered the truth of this for myself in Tehran in 2009. I was in Iran researching a book (*Saved by Beauty*) in which I hoped to show the human face of a culture that was known in the West as part of "the axis of evil." On leaving the country, I was stopped at the airport by members of the Iranian security services and taken back to Tehran for questioning. They took me to the very same hotel in which I had been staying, ushered me into a back-door service elevator that took me up to the top floor, and showed me into a suite overlooking the city below.

For the next two days, they questioned me over and over on my reasons for being in Iran and made it clear they considered me a spy. They also showed me that they had listened to every phone call and seen all my emails. They slept round my bed and continued with their questions as soon as I had woken. Finally, they said I had the choice of either going to Evin Prison for several years or agreeing to work for them. They wanted me to report on the activities of foreign nongovernmental organizations in Iran. If I agreed, they would let me go. I agreed. They left the room, saying they would be back in five minutes.

They didn't come back for an hour or more, and in that time I could feel the story of my life as I knew it slipping away. For all I knew, I would never see the outside world again, my friends and family, or the city I had grown to love, San Francisco. I would perhaps never write the book I had come to Tehran to write. And yet the strange thing was, I was not afraid. Something in me began to see my life's story for what it was—as just that, a story. If the story was interrupted, another story would inevitably take its place—prisoner in Tehran, wrongfully accused of spying—until all stories ended with my death.

But in the meantime, I became aware, as I had never quite done before, of an aliveness, a quality of being, that was silently humming along all the while, whatever story it might be cloaked in. In that moment I knew for certain, and not with my thinking mind, that whatever changes my story might go through, I would continue to be a living, breathing presence of aliveness that permeated all my days.

It wasn't that I didn't care what happened. Of course I cared. I wanted to be on the next plane out. But the question of what the future might hold no longer weighed on me like a dark cloud as it had begun to do when the security agents first left the room. Something had lifted. Recognizing that I was utterly helpless and unable to do anything to change my circumstances, something in me let go. I let go of all hope, all despair, and all struggle. I gave up. And that was when I felt as alive and present to the world as I had ever felt. In that hour, the Iranian security service gave me the gift of a taste of freedom.

Evidently, I returned to tell the tale. My familiar story continues, and no, I do not work for the Iranian security or intelligence services. Neither do I always live today at the frequency I realized in that hotel room in Tehran. But it left its mark on me, and though everything appears the same, I inhabit it differently somehow—more lightly, perhaps, though I can't count on it.

Change can usher in a new life. It hardly needs to be dramatic in the way my Tehran experience was. People like me may need a hammer to break through their encrustations, while others need only a feather. It may simply require looking up one day instead of down and suddenly seeing, for no reason, the world and oneself through a different lens.

But whatever kind of change provides the catalyst, a new life will always require a death of some kind; otherwise it is nothing new, but rather a shuffling of the same deck. What we die to is an outworn way of being in the world. We experience ourselves differently. We are no longer who we thought we were. But I do not suggest for one moment that letting go of an outworn story is easy, nor are there any guarantees. Change can open the door to a new road. But if you start down a new road, you cannot, by definition, know where it will take you.

All the same, when you are ready, you begin. The directness of this knowing, quiet yet strong, can propel you out of your habitual perceptions of life and into the unknown before you even have a moment to think about it. It is a dawning of a deeper realization from some other domain that is an intrinsic part of the human experience. Poets in all ages have caught the glimmer of it. Rilke, in one of his early poems, speaks of a man who gets up without warning in the middle of a meal

> and walks outdoors, and keeps on walking,
> because of a church that stands somewhere
> in the East. ☙

When the man in Rilke's poem drops out of his life and walks outdoors, he isn't acting on a decision he had made a week beforehand. He knows that the time for change has come, and now is the time to act on it. He does not make the decision to walk. It isn't premeditated. One day he just knows; so his walking is effortless, as simple as breathing. When we just know like that, then whatever happens next is effortless. There is nothing to do other than to follow the thread of our life that we can feel between our fingers. All of a sudden, Rilke's man lets go of an identity he may have been carrying for years. This is the real change, the transformational change that awaits our recognition within the changes that take place in any human life. He walks into the unknown, into a new life, without any apparent useful purpose whatsoever.

He assents to the realization that everything has conspired to make this the only thing he can do. The action unfolds out of the clarity and stillness of a knowing heart. In that stillness, there is nothing to do but to trust the change, wherever it takes us; nothing to do but walk right down the middle between hope and fear into the *wow* of the life that is waiting for us, whatever it may be.

6

Trust the Imperfection

∾

And the golden bees
were making white combs
and sweet honey
from my old failures.
ANTONIO MACHADO,
FROM "LAST NIGHT AS I WAS SLEEPING"

It was Sir Thomas More who first popularized the term *Utopia*, in his book of that name, published in 1516. But although the word has been commonly used for at least five hundred years, few people today realize that the original Greek comprises *U*, meaning "not," and *topia*, meaning "a place," which is to say that the ideal place or situation does not and cannot ever exist. Even so, as individuals and as societies, we continue as ever to think that the perfect way of life does exist somewhere and that one day our lives will have everything in place and the heavenly city will shine here on Earth, at least in our little corner, if not everywhere else.

We might wonder then why it is that so many utopian movements have ended not only in tragedy, but also in the very opposite of their lofty ideals. It is not only religious movements that descend into fanaticism in order to spread their own version of a perfect world for everyone. The French and Russian revolutions, equally horrific, were both secular, antireligious tides. The American invasion of Iraq may serve as a more recent example of a utopian ideal gone wrong. Inspired by the neoconservative conviction that American democracy is the ideal social model for everyone, it resulted in tens of thousands of deaths and no democracy at all, American or otherwise.

You might say that political idealism is different; that it always involves individuals driven by insatiable power needs who will use any means to justify their ends. But the same tendency toward entropy—the dispersion and eventual disintegration of what were originally fine and even noble ideals and aspirations—can happen in the most apparently benign of situations. Think of Brook Farm, the utopian community founded in the 1840s in Massachusetts. It drew its inspiration from the Transcendentalist movement, whose leading lights were Emerson and Thoreau. The writer Nathaniel Hawthorne was one of its founding members. Everyone, women and men, was paid equally for their labors on the farm and in their school. The motive was to have a balance of labor and leisure that enabled all members to work together for the benefit of the greater community—noble ideals indeed. But it took no more than five or six years and a bad fire to set the members against each other and for the community to disintegrate. The same pattern happened over and over in the spiritual and religious communities that mushroomed in the 1960s.

The film *Pleasantville* (1998) tackles this theme in a sobering and sometimes chilling way. A 1950s community where everyone is deliberately pleasant, where there is no crime and the fire department's only job is to rescue cats from trees, seems like the perfect place to live. But it all starts to disintegrate when a girl breaks ranks and has sex before marriage. The act unleashes not only sexual feelings, but feelings in general—joy, anger, indignation, appreciation for beauty—which had always been kept hidden beneath a veneer of normalcy and order. Freud would have had a field day in Pleasantville.

If, however, the perfect life seems to be unattainable on Earth, then clearly the next best thing is to kick the can into heaven. Everything will be perfect there, after we are dead, and it can be perfect even while we are alive, if we can only fix our attention with single-mindedness on that great perfection. In this view, our purpose here is to turn our back on earthly delights and ascend via a Ladder of Perfection to that celestial condition of being that no longer needs a "Do Not Disturb" sign, because all disturbances only happen here below.

Plato was the first protagonist of the Ladder of Perfection idea, and it has had a long history of adherents ever since. The Cathars were a gnostic Christian sect of the twelfth and thirteenth centuries whose leaders called themselves "the Perfect," walked around in white, had the merely "good" people provide them with food because the earth was too evil for them to put their hands into, and didn't have sex because it would be a sin to bring another human being into the fallen condition of a physical life. The Cathars were all slaughtered for their faith by other Christians, led by another holy man, Saint Bernard, who was obsessed by the danger he thought the Cathars posed to the one true church. After all, they dared to denounce the loose morals of the Catholic clergy of the time and did not recognize the sacraments.

Christianity is littered with individuals who bent and contorted their bodies and minds in pursuit of perfection. Saint

Simeon removed himself from the daily world by spending much of his life standing on a tall pillar, doubtless at some cost to his legs. Sir (or Saint) Thomas More, like so many of his contemporaries, would use a scourge on himself and wear a hair shirt to ensure the body and its appetites knew who was in charge.

It is ironic too that while More enshrined religious tolerance and pluralism in the Utopia he describes in his book, in real life he used his authority as Archbishop of Canterbury to torture and disembowel anyone whom he suspected of holding beliefs different in any degree from orthodox Catholicism. So convinced was he of the righteousness of his position that he gave up his life for it when he refused to acknowledge Henry VIII rather than the pope as the head of the church in England.

This is the thing with martyrs: you may admire their resolve and their conviction in their beliefs, but it is difficult to ignore the blinders they set over their eyes in their desperate pursuit of being the good person, the good wife, the good father, the good employee (after all, martyrs do not appear only in religious clothing). Any struggle toward the perfect, in whatever sphere of human existence, necessitates a narrowing of focus that sees life according to a specific set of standards, which must be followed whatever the cost to oneself or to others. For a perfectionist, to neglect those standards would be to invite guilt, self-denigration, feelings of worthlessness and inadequacy, and even, in extreme circumstances, self-harm. Anorexia and bulimia can both be traced to the rigors of the perfectionist ideal and the self-hatred that can occur when one doesn't measure up to one's own standards.

Freud coined the term *superego* for the conglomerate of attitudes, learned early in life, that are internalized and shaped into an authority figure who sits somewhere behind the brow and attempts to rule from on high—an internalized Jehovah, you could say, whose more kindly manifestation might be the policeman. Perfectionists set themselves up in judgment of themselves and, by extension, of everyone else whom they perceive to fall short of their standards. The superego's primary function is to damp down any tendency that might threaten the order and apparent coherence of the identity one has constructed upon a rigid worldview.

Sex, drugs, and rock and roll will always be the first to go if the superego has its way. Yet we know from historical precedent that the great Dionysius, god of excess, wine, and song, will never be kept under wraps for long. After the 1950s came the '60s. But neither will peace ever reign for long. Despite all the best efforts of the superego, there will always be some discord somewhere, both personally and culturally. We will never conform to any ideal of a perfect life, however hard we try. And the more we try, the more unhappy and frustrated we will become. There are more than enough taut mothers, striving husbands, desperate housewives, and angry, obedient children around to prove it.

We are imperfect beings. This is our truth. Yet we do everything we can to erase that fact and improve ourselves on the lines of some model we have signed up to—a model we have seen in the magazines; discovered in a spiritual tradition or in a political or social movement that our parents bequeathed to us or that the latest celebrities have reflected back to us.

Striving to match the standards of these models is not exactly a new phenomenon. Young Greeks were working out two and a half thousand years ago. In the sixteenth century, Montaigne wrote that he had seen some French women "swallow sand and ashes, and work deliberately to ruin their stomach, so as to get pale complexions. To get a slim body, Spanish style, what torture do they not endure, tight-laced and braced, until they suffer great gashes in their sides, right to the live flesh—yes, sometimes even until they die of it."

Very few of us are perfect specimens of the physical human form, and the irony is that the cultural ideal of the perfect body changes anyway with the generations. Marilyn Monroe wouldn't make *Vogue* in the twenty-first century. We all have our physical imperfections when compared with some standard model, and many of these imperfections we share with most everyone else. Breasts are too small, thighs are too thick, cheeks are too plump—there's always something not quite right.

But today, unlike in de Montaigne's time, if you don't like the body you have, you can go so far as to change it almost beyond recognition. Will it be just a matter of time before the same is true of genetically modified minds?

Welcome to the world of the enhanced human being. Botox and Viagra will seem quaint in a few years' time. The ethical and philosophical debate on GMHs—genetically modified humans—has barely begun, but it will doubtless command a great deal of attention and interest in the decades to come. After all, if you were offered a math-gene implant, or a compassion-gene implant, or a generosity-gene implant, would you reject it out of hand? Wouldn't this be a better world if we were all fitted out with compassion genes or greater discernment abilities? These questions are no longer the preserve of science fiction, and they deserve serious reflection.

Gary Shteyngart, in his novel *Super Sad True Love Story* (2010), the latest in the *Brave New World* genre, describes an America in the near future whose culture is divided between the enhanced—the technologically wired (wired into your brain)—and the naturals, the technologically disadvantaged. Lenny, the main character, sells immortality packages to the superrich, immortality being the ultimate fantasy for those who have the means to improve their lot. After all, the fear of extinction is probably the engine driving the perfectionism project in the first place.

The greatest loss in an enhanced culture would surely be the freedom to consciously choose your responses. If you are programmed to be compassionate, it follows that your compassion would be unconscious and automatic, rather than an individual choice made with awareness. How then could we open into the *knowing field* that we are? Compassion would no longer be a natural expression of our deeper nature, but merely a knee-jerk reaction. It would be absent the quality of presence and knowing. The whole improvement model is based on a materialistic and mechanical view of the human being, one in which there is no deeper awareness than that of the conscious ego, its needs and preferences. The notion of a nonphysical dimension of being in which we partake of reality as a whole through a movement of intentional awareness—our essential humanity—would become irrelevant.

In essence, our desire to improve ourselves is predicated on our dissatisfaction with who we think we are. We are beset by limitations: physical limitations, mental limitations, and limitations of character. Our limitations are inherent to human existence, and no amount of scientific development will mitigate that fact, despite the genetic tinkering that fills so many research labs now. No amount of self-affirmations and positive thinking will change the reality either.

Those same limitations—our imperfections—are seen differently by those who do not swallow the materialist model of existence. Carl Jung, in *The Red Book*, writes,

> The one who has learned to live with his incapacity has
> learned a great deal. This will lead us to the valuation

of the smallest things, and to wise limitation, which the greater height demands . . . The heroic in you is the fact that you are ruled by the thought that this or that is good, that this or that performance is indispensable, this or that cause is objectionable, this or that goal must be attained in headlong striving work, this or that pleasure should be ruthlessly repressed at all costs. Consequently, you sin against incapacity. But incapacity exists. No one should deny it, find fault with it, or shout it down. ✍

It is precisely our limitations that make each of us human and also the unique individuals that we are. Being limited and imperfect, we can count on making mistakes. However cautious and responsible we may be, mistakes are still bound to happen anyway. They are unavoidable. We take the wrong job, we choose the wrong partner, we bet on the wrong horse, we buy when we should have sold, we have one drink too many.

But then can we ever be sure that mistakes are really mistakes? After all, we can never fully know the true outcome of any course of action. Mistakes have led to the discovery of DNA, penicillin, aspirin, X-rays, Teflon, Velcro, nylon, cornflakes, Coca-Cola, chocolate chip cookies, and more. But there may be an even deeper elegance latent in error—deeper than the fact that mistakes give us opportunities to learn. Our mistakes and our limitations also give us the opportunity to embrace ourselves exactly as we are—not to identify solely with our moments of clear awareness, but to accept the whole picture, blemishes and all.

What Jung calls "the heroic" in the passage quoted above is the ego that strives toward some form of perfection—spiritual, material, or both. The hero divides the world into good and bad, right and wrong. He strives for the light and pushes away the darkness. He strives for purity and rejects anything that might tarnish his glow. But if we can trust that our imperfections are part of our humanness—that they are not to be rejected, but seen and acknowledged as part of our life in this human form—then our relationship with ourselves can soften, become kinder, and we will see ourselves in a warmer light. In embracing all that we can see of ourselves, the dark as well as the light, our imperfections are redeemed somehow and can even take on the robe of beauty.

Not that the embrace and the redemption are painless: self-knowledge is a sobering process. It involves disillusionment, a dismantling of the images and ideas we have had about who we are. Self-knowledge is precisely the purging that happens in Purgatory, as Dante discovers on his journey through the other worlds. Our imperfections are transformed from within, in the light of our own compassionate and accepting regard, rather than by some plan of action imposed by the mind alone.

Can we confess to what we see in the mirror, as Dante did in the dark wood? Can we accept the journey into our own darkness, where we may be ground to pieces by the reality we are faced with (*contrition* derives from the Latin *tero*, "I grind")? From this a new attitude can dawn, in which meaningless suffering is transformed into the conscious and intentional acknowledgment of our condition. Yet the regard is a tender one, accepting as it is of our own vulnerabilities, and its non-judgmental inclusivity can lead us to the essence of who we are—to at-one-ment.

That same tender regard, that wholehearted, holistic way of looking at people, can lead us to the essence of who someone else is. Susanne is the grandmother of a Down syndrome child. She is in my writing group, and in a piece on her granddaughter, she wrote,

Before Sadie came into my life, I couldn't easily relate
to people with developmental disabilities. Theirs was a
foreign world to me. Now, when I see someone with Down
Syndrome I feel like running up to them and giving them a
big hug. I live in a much bigger world now. ❧

Susanne asked her daughter, Heidi, if she would write a para-
graph about Sadie. This is what Sadie's mother wrote:

If I had to describe Sadie in one word it would be "perfect."
Sadie doesn't look like my other kids, but her beauty exudes
from her every pore and makes her a beauty queen. I call
her my koala bear because when she hugs you it's a whole
body hug—arms and legs wrapped around you. It's bliss. I
could watch her all day. I stare into those beady little eyes
and wonder what her world is like and how she experiences
life. She's pleasured by the simplest activities: drawing circles,
dancing, cuddling, and singing. She's always so proud of
herself. I will never forget the first time she walked. She was
entirely overtaken with joy when she finally did it. Sadie has
to work hard to learn. I took for granted how easy it comes to
typical children to walk, talk, sit—most everything in Sadie's
world takes more time and patience. She's taught me to get
out of the race. I just love her and don't know how I would be
without her. I often think if I could go back in time and plan
my future, I'd plan Sadie exactly how she is now—perfect. ❧

Far from denying the fact of Sadie's developmental disabilities,
her mother sees the perfection in her daughter's imperfect form.
Seen through the eyes of love, Sadie's "beauty exudes from every
pore." Sadie *fits* in her family perfectly. Utterly accepted for who
she is, she can be at home in herself and with others. Isn't that

what we all long for in the end, the feeling of being at home in ourselves and in this world?

William James distinguished between what he called the once-born and the twice-born. The once-born are those who do not question existence and live out their lives with contentment. They are at home in themselves and in the world because they do not wonder why. It's as if someone gave them a happiness gene. The twice-born are aware of their failings and the sufferings of life, and they long for a harmony that seems unattainable in this world. Unsatisfied with the palliatives that the world can offer—wealth, fame, success, a beautiful mind or body—and all too conscious of their failings and vulnerabilities, they set out on their own journey of self-discovery, only to realize finally that what they are looking for has been there all along. They have been looking for home. They want to feel a *fit* in their lives, that everything connects. Rumi says that

> This longing you express
> Is the return message. ❧

The *fit*, the *connection,* happens when we finally come home to who we are in our entirety. Embracing our sadness, our grief, our aging body as well as our joys and inspirations—embracing everything that we are—Rumi tells us, *is* the way home. The deep acceptance—not a grudging acceptance but a celebration—of who we are is the beginning of the cure for spiritual homesickness. The more we can settle into our fullness, into an awareness and acceptance of the full range of our humanity, the more we can open to "the transcendent function," as Jung called it—the third force, which I have called the *knowing field.* As the Indian sage Shivapuri Baba once said, "If you can't free yourself from like and dislike, you might as well join a religion."

In Japan there is an entire worldview that appreciates the value of the imperfect, unfinished, and faulty. It's called *wabi-sabi*. *Wabi* refers to something simple and unpretentious, and *sabi* points to the beauty that comes with age. Wabi-sabi is the aesthetic view that underlies traditional Japanese art forms like the tea ceremony, calligraphy, and ceramics. It's an aesthetic that sees beauty in the modest and humble, the irregular and earthy. It sees beauty in the wear that comes from age and use. The imperfect is understood and valued for its contribution to a truthful portrayal of life.

The same understanding was common in most traditional cultures. The old carpet weavers of Central Asia and Iran would always make a small but deliberate "mistake" in their design—the pattern in one corner not quite matching that in the opposite corner, or a color being a slightly different tone at either end of the carpet. Perfection, these old Muslim cultures held, was the prerogative of God, not human beings. Including an imperfection in their work was an act of humility. It acknowledged the limitations that come with the simple fact of being human. Moreover, the older the carpet was, the more it was valued and prized.

How different this view is from our cultural obsession with the new and the fresh, above all else. We long to live in a perpetual springtime, in which not only the body but also the mind retains all its spring and tone for the length of a lifetime. When reality intervenes, we spirit the elderly out of sight, away to the departure lounge of a retirement home.

It has not always been so. Traditional societies valued the contribution their elders could make to younger generations and honored their elders accordingly. Artists have long been fascinated with the subject of old age, but it was Rembrandt who made the painting of the elderly a lifelong passion. He painted old people from the time he was twenty until months before he died. Age spots, wrinkled hands, the lines of experience, the lifetime you can see in an older person's eyes—these were for him the marks of a soul's passage through life. He was captivated more by the qualities that he saw in an old person's face than all the untested beauty of youth.

All the sorrows and kindnesses, joys and tragedies that marked Rembrandt's own life are there for all to see in his self-portraits. When I first saw him in the National Gallery in London, his eyes seemed to reach out and draw me toward him from the other side of the room. They were the eyes of an old man whose rumpled face glowed against a background of darkness.

There was no disguising either his age or his mood. It wasn't that he was resigned or melancholy. He was so fully present to the truth of his condition, so unapologetically who he was, that he summoned something of the same in me. "This is how I look," those eyes seemed to say. "This is who I am, no nips no tucks." In seeing into the core of himself, this man was letting me in on a secret about my own life—secret only because I hadn't known to look in the way he had. We are aging, we are dying; we are full of sorrow, full of feeling, full of life; we are beautiful, however we look. We are who we are. My own face is enough, he tells me, if I can dare, like him, to look in the mirror and see into the layers that are there. Infinite layers, waves of the sea. We are finite and infinite and everything in between. I walked up to the frame. "Rembrandt van Rijn," it said. "Self-Portrait. 1669," the year of his death.

Day by day, tiny specks of us float away. Nothing will dispel the reality that we are not built to last. Death is our ultimate limitation, the final proof that perfection was never meant to be part of the human experience. Sooner rather than later we shall not be here: no eyes, no nose, no ears, no tongue, no mind, no you or me—gone, and who knows where?

Can we trust even this? The not knowing what lies on the other side of death's door? Can we say, with Mary Oliver, that

I want to step through the door full of curiosity, wondering: what is it going to be like, that cottage of darkness? ✑

Feeling our soon-not-to-be-hereness in our bones may be the best motivation we have for waking up to the miracle that we are here now at all. It prompts Mary Oliver, in that same poem, "When Death Comes," to see everything around her as "a brotherhood and a sisterhood," and to see both the commonality and uniqueness in every living thing. And if you think about it, that is the brilliance of the human design plan—the built-in "defect" is the very thing that can spur us to taste fully the moment we are living now.

7

Trust the Letting Go

You need not leave your room. Remain seated at
your table and listen. You need not even listen;
simply wait. You need not even wait; just be
quiet, still, and solitary. The world will freely
offer itself to you to be unmasked. It has no
choice; it will roll in ecstasy at your feet.

FRANZ KAFKA

Rilke's man who gets up from the dinner table and walks
outside, at the end of the "Trust the Changes" chapter,
and then keeps on walking, has probably disappeared
by now into the true life that had been waiting for him all along.
Rilke makes it sound so easy. But surely his man must have
been practicing for years before suddenly walking out doors
and never looking back? You know, deep meditation, solitary
retreats, lots of therapy, that sort of thing.

If you want to play the piano, you practice. Tennis cham-
pion Roger Federer practices his serve. Buddhists practice

gazing at a white wall or dreaming up images of gods and goddesses who sit on the crown of their head and dissolve into them. Christians practice centering prayer—or some of them do, anyway. There are hundreds of useful spiritual practices, and you will probably have preferences of your own. Practice trains the brain, lays down tracks that lead us where we want to go. Practice makes perfect. But perfection, remember, is not all it's cracked up to be.

We live in a world where everyone is busy trying to be someone. If you want to be someone, you have to practice the skill sets you need to get you there. If you want to be spiritual, then you have to do what is necessary in whichever way suits your temperament. There is no question that practice has value, but not if you are using it in a spiritual context to try to get somewhere or to improve yourself. After all, the idea of most spiritual practice is ultimately to dissolve the practitioner. If that is what you really want, then your desire is not to be spiritual but to be invisible—not to have a special robe to signify your spiritual attainment, not to disappear into the delights of your own psyche, nor even to retire from the world, but to live in this world so lightly that, like Keats, you can say on your tombstone, "Here lies one whose name was writ on water."

We have become so culturally addicted to doing, to getting somewhere and becoming someone, that the same tendency bleeds over into spiritual life. Even relaxation, the quintessential doing nothing, is something you have to practice, and seriously, in a class for which the time slot is logged into your diary.

The importance of staying busy is a Protestant obsession that America inherited from Northern Europe and has since tuned to a fine art. The more hours you spend in the office, the more multitasking you do, the fewer vacations you take, the more professional you are, the more your social credibility increases in stock. You are a good, productive, and useful person if your diary is crammed for the foreseeable future.

This is the cultural context we live and breathe. So it's not surprising to think that when you are not working on your career—why, that's no reason to be idle—you can work on yourself! You can get a fitter, leaner body, a more balanced mind, a cleaner spirit. Not only psychological but also spiritual success is just the next frontier when the world's achievements begin to pall.

Carl Jung, among many others, suggests another way:

> You teem with intentions and desirousness! Do you still
> not know that the way to truth stands open only to those
> without intentions? . . . Letting things happen, the action
> through non-action, the letting go of oneself of Meister
> Eckhart, became the key for me that succeeded in opening
> the door to the way: One must be able to psychically let
> things happen. ﹏

This is inflammatory. It flies in the face of dozens of best-selling advice and self-help books and the conventional wisdom of our times. If you don't have intention, then you are a loser drifting around in your daydreams. You need a purpose-driven life. You need goals and strategies to achieve them. After all, how could we survive without them? We would never get anywhere, never get anything done.

Even to consider such a prospect can open up a chasm beneath our feet. It's not pleasant to feel like a donut with a hole in the middle. So we juggle balls in the air as fast as possible, and we hope no one can see the empty spaces, the nothing, between them. Nothing can be really frightening. Feeling invisible is another way of saying we feel we are nothing, nobody, with no existence or value to speak of. And the emptiness is there because it is real, though not in the scary way the ego envisions it. A friendlier term would be "the feeling of one's existence as spaciousness." We are so spacious, so undefined by form, that we can never locate precisely where and who we are. We are ungraspable, a curl of mist on the wind, an unutterable mystery even to ourselves.

Becoming ungraspable is the eventual aim of all spiritual practices, even if they are not advertised as such. They are meant to lead us into the empty spaciousness that we are—the very spaciousness that busyness is so effective at disguising, at least for a while. Along the way, however, the ego can imperceptibly turn practices into another form of doing, becoming, in their turn, a substitute for the very no-thingness they are designed to lead toward. In that way, we can take on the identity of a proficient meditator or spiritual practitioner, someone with spiritual experiences under his or her belt, rather than the fluid identity of one whose name is "writ on water."

You probably have some practices of your own already, and they are doubtless of use to you. But for now, instead of practices, let's consider a general orientation, one that can encourage rest instead of effort, being rather than doing, whatever we may or may not be doing—a disposition that is resonant and synchronous with the spacious field that we are.

A fully lived life is not dependent on what we do or on whether we deem it to be worthwhile or not. It is about the sheer simplicity of being. Being what? That we shall discover only when we rest awhile from being everything that we think we are, including being a meditator or a spiritual practitioner.

"Negative capability" was the term the poet John Keats used for this capacity to let go of all willful trying, however subtle it may be. It is essential, he said, to have periods of empty space in one's life to allow creative ideas to surface. In 1818, he wrote these lines in a letter to his friend J. H. Reynolds:

> Let us not therefore go hurrying about and collecting honey-bee like, buzzing here and there impatiently for a knowledge of what is to be arrived at; but let us open our leaves like a flower, and be passive and receptive—budding patiently under the eye of Apollo and taking hints from every noble insect that favors us with a visit. ✍

Every spiritual tradition recognizes that the mind needs to come to rest to reflect the clear light of being. Once, in India, I met a man who said that all that was needed was to park the body somewhere and do nothing else but sit still for a while. Don't try and sit still, he said. Don't force yourself into a posture that will make you sit still. Relax, and stay awake and attentive in the relaxation. If you don't you will fall into a stupor, which is not relaxation but its caricature. Be kind to yourself. Take your time. Don't try and meditate. No technique is necessary; just let yourself relax mindfully and deeply into the present moment that manifests as the simple sensation of your body sitting there.

On another visit to India, I went to visit Veerupaksha Cave, on Mount Arunachala in Tamil Nadu. The great saint of the mid-twentieth century, Ramana Maharshi, had lived in this cave for sixteen years in silence and solitude. A notice at the cave entrance asked visitors to keep silence. There were three pairs of shoes outside the entrance. I left my shoes alongside them and passed through a vestibule hung with pictures of Ramana into the darkness of the cave itself. Three people were sitting motionless in front of a stone ledge. On the ledge, just discernible in the light of a tiny oil lamp, was an elongated mound draped in a faded yellow cloth and a flower garland. I sat down on the floor near the others. The air was hot and thick. Just sitting there, the silence and the stillness began to enter my mind.

It was a relief to be in the darkness after the glare of the sun. I sensed the wisdom of those builders of old Romanesque churches, which in Europe I had so often passed by in favor of the radiance and soaring of their Gothic successors. This cave, like one of those early churches, was a womb. Its darkness felt to me to be the darkness of not knowing, of some secret germination beyond the aspirations or grasp of the daylight mind. Maybe I was there for an hour or so, when out of nowhere a voice suddenly rang through the quiet of my body: "Just rest," it said. "Just rest."

I don't know where those words came from. They were both inside me and outside, in the cave, at the same time. I had thought that I was already at rest. Barely a thought had passed through my mind in the time I had been there. But as I heard these words, I was instantly aware of the subtle effort I had been making all along to be aware of the silence I was in. Even that effort was a residual holding back from being there, where I was, in utter simplicity—a degree of separation in the form of a subtle observer, an observer who remained a ripple on the surface of consciousness.

Something let go in me then. The dark cave took me, and in that moment, it was as if the mountain itself moved through me. In that moment, the life of the mountain, the cave, and my own innermost being became one and the same thing. Later, I realized that I had glimpsed how, in its deepest reaches, relaxation is a profound letting go of any effort or intention at all. At its heart, it is a letting go of the ego altogether, a dissolution into the endless reaches of Being.

The simplicity of just being is resonant with the cultural sensibility of old India, the one that existed before call centers and software startups. Old India is still there in places, and it can be here too, wherever you are. You don't have to go to India to know the meaning of stillness, to stop trying to get it right, whatever right is. Starbucks or your local café will do. Only don't rush in and get a cup to go. (The to-go cup, by the way, is inconceivable around the Mediterranean, which is still a far less utilitarian culture than ours. The value of the café, apart from the cappuccino, is that it offers you a place where you can sit and happily do nothing in the company of others, most of whom, if they are not on their laptops, are also doing nothing more useful than sipping coffee and looking at each other.)

Here where we are, wherever we are, we can gently bring our attention to the aliveness of our bodily form—the feel of the chair we are sitting on, the taste of the coffee as it slips through our lips, the passing show of the other customers—but from a place of stillness, from a rested and awake mind, knowing we do not have to be anywhere but where we are now or doing anything other than what we are doing now. Then the present moment can replace our daydreams and the hurried procession of undigested thoughts. We can know a quiet gladness, a sense of breadth and spaciousness that is made possible by dropping for a while our story of who we think we are. No matter what we are doing or not doing, true rest happens when we take a rest from ourselves. When that happens, we are naturally awake and aware.

However, you may not be a café person. You may have your own ways of taking a rest from yourself, apart from the meditation hall. The hammock did it for the poet James Wright. He wrote a whole poem about it. Lying there, he was aware of the bronze butterfly over his head, an empty house, the cowbells, a chicken hawk, and the evening darkness coming on. Then his poem ends with this shocking line: "I have wasted my life."

What does Wright mean by that? He has just described this idyllic scene, viewed from out of the side of a swaying hammock, and now he says he has wasted his life!

He means that he realizes, lying there, that this doing nothing for no good reason is the most alive and vital thing he knows. And yet he hardly ever lets himself fall into it. Like all of us, he is usually too preoccupied with earning a living, caring for a family, and everything else that fills our days. He echoes this last line in another poem when he writes,

> I want to lie down under a tree.
> This is the only duty that is not death. ✍

Wright knew that given the opportunity, the cells of the body can settle into their rightful place, in harmony with the living world. The mind itself can become clear instead of clouded, as still as a lake with no wind. When we take time out from the busy mind, we will know why Wright felt strongly enough to write that last line. Can we allow ourselves this small gift? Can we feel free to lie in the grass for a while and feel the life we have been given? Can we say, like the eighth-century Chinese poet Li Po,

> Naked I lie in the green forest of summer . . .
> Too lazy to wave my white feathered fan.
> I hang my cap on a crag,
> And bare my head to the wind that comes
> Blowing through the pine trees. ✍

Yet you do not have to lie down in the grass or in a hammock to let go of the habitual "buzzing here and there," as Keats called it. Being still inside does not necessarily mean being immobile, just as the capacity to let go and do nothing ultimately has nothing to do with what you are doing or not doing. You can be lying on the beach and be furiously working schemes, daydreams, or sexual fantasies. On the other hand, you can be conducting an orchestra or playing tennis and be so fully in the experience that the notion of conscious will falls away, and it feels like you are doing nothing at all. You can be dancing as Rumi danced or turning a potter's wheel the way the Zen masters did. You have forgotten yourself, let go of yourself, and then whatever you are doing—whether it be making love, mowing the lawn, or writing a poem—seems to be doing itself somehow, from out of a center of stillness.

Writing, dancing, painting, making music—any act of sustained attention can lead us into the feeling of our own existence, into the stillness and the silence that we always are beneath the flurry and scurry of worries and hopes and thoughts that all too often fill our days. Forgetting ourselves, we find ourselves. That's when we remember the wisdom that Chuang Tzu packs into these lines:

> The right way to go easy
> Is to forget the right way
> And forget that the going is easy. ॐ

We can also walk ourselves into stillness. Walking, not as a regimen—nor with a cell phone—but as an engagement with the living world, quiets the mind. Something lets go in us after walking our way through the natural world. We feel refreshed, not only because of the physical exercise, but also because of the return to ourselves that walking can foster.

Why did monks used to wander? Why do so many modern-day secular pilgrims, most of them without the spur of a religious faith, still walk the old ways wherever they can be found—in France, in Italy, and especially the Camino de Santiago de Compostela in Spain? Almost one hundred fifty thousand people, of all ages and from more than a hundred countries, walked the Camino in 2011, and each will have his or her own answer to that question. But in their own words and understanding, each of those answers is likely to have something to do with the person becoming closer to, more intimate with, him- or herself and his or her life.

"I only went out for a walk," John Muir said, "and finally concluded to stay out til sundown, for going out, I found, was really going in."

"They give me joy as I proceed," wrote the nineteenth-century English poet John Clare of the old footpaths of his local land.

William Wordsworth, in the final months of the eighteenth century, tramped across the Pennine Hills of his native Northern England not on some religious pilgrimage or out of any necessity, but for the sheer pleasure of it. He thereby started a revolution in our relationship both with ourselves and with nature that has continued to this day. Before then, people would walk because they had to, and the middle and upper classes never had to.

Wordsworth started a fashion among literary and educated types: walking solely for the pleasure of one's own company and for charting one's personal thoughts, emotions, and reflections on the beauty of nature along the way. It is often said that the birth of the novel in the eighteenth century was the catalyst for the value we now give to subjective experience, but it was, in fact, Wordsworth and his fellow Romantic poets who, more than anyone, gave credibility to the interior world that can come alive while walking.

In 1815, Wordsworth wrote of how one can access "the depths of reason" while walking. He called these depths "a profound realm to which the mind cannot sink gently of itself—but to which it must descend by treading the steps of thought." I like to think he was speaking of the conscious, knowing self behind thoughts. Wordsworth strode thousands of miles all over England and Europe as a young man, composing his poems along the way. His "depths of reason" went beyond ordinary thought to the wordless contemplation from which great poetry is born. Wandering "lonely as a cloud" over hill and dale, Wordsworth wrote *The Prelude,* an entire autobiography in verse, from the fruits of his strollings.

Throughout my own adult life, for nearly thirty years, I have regularly dropped my ordinary routine and gone wandering in remote and untamed places of the world, or taken myself off along some traditional pilgrimage route. Yet it has always been at a leisurely pace, a dawdle even, with plenty of time to stand and stare. I am not an explorer or an intrepid adventurer. Nor can I lay claim to being a pilgrim in the traditional sense of the word, since I do not affiliate myself with any religion. I love to walk because it returns me to the stillness that comes with walking.

For ancient peoples—the aborigines of Australia, the native Indians of the Americas—walking and knowing were almost synonymous terms. In the language of the Klinchon people of northwestern Canada, the terms for "knowledge" and for "footprint" can be used interchangeably. The origin of our own verb *to learn* has its roots in the Proto-Germanic word meaning "to follow a track."

The knowledge we come to when walking is first and foremost of ourselves. Walking, not as a regimen but as an engagement with oneself and the living world, quiets the mind. And in that quiet we can come first and foremost to a deeper knowledge of ourselves. This is what can happen for me now when I walk round my local mountain, Mount Tamalpais in Marin County, just two and a half thousand feet high, as it can for you on your own favorite walk. After a while, flocks of thoughts can disappear into the blue, and the sheer joy that John Clare spoke of can rise up with every footfall. More often the walking is sober; a quiet and abiding peace emerges, and I know that, whatever problems my mind may have wanted some answer to, all is well with the world. Walking is so ordinary. But then, the stillness we are is ordinary—ordinary, and marvelous too.

8

Keep Faith with Beauty

సా

Mankind will be saved by beauty.
FYODOR DOSTOEVSKY

Beauty lifts my gaze. It does. It did this morning. I'm puffing up the side of Mount Tam, my heart blowing and clanking like an old steam engine, and I'm thinking I can't have much more to go, in life I mean, if a small incline reduces me to a shadow of myself like this. But then what am I going to do if I . . . I look up, and there in the distance, the city of San Francisco hovers and floats on the bay under strands of gray mist, and the usual bright blue of the Californian sky is softened and modulated with trailing wisps of autumn vapor that stretch their lengthy banners over Berkeley, and three Canada geese wheel honking to the left and curve into space before dipping below the madrones and the redwoods that forest the canyon falling away to the east below me. I stop, I look, my concerns fall away, and I stand there, flushed with gratitude for the beauty of existence.

"Think of all the beauty around you and be happy," Anne Frank wrote. She should know the value of beauty, if anyone does. Anne Frank was sixteen when she died in Bergen-Belsen concentration camp. Before she died, she must have known, she must have seen, to be able to say such a thing in those darkest of hours—to say that matter can be illuminated and clarified by a quality of grace beyond its merely material form, beyond even circumstances that would normally be considered so horrific as to be unredeemable. Matter transformed—either of itself or in the light of our imagination—opens our hearts and minds and joins us to the living miracle of the world.

At the heart of beauty is the union of spirit and matter. Spirit: the ineffable, ungraspable quality that brings something alive. Beauty: a unity beyond rational apprehension, a whole greater than the sum of its parts, a lens or a window that offers a glimpse of a greater dimension of reality, one that brings us closer to the source of being. Beauty was the window that was open to me on my way up Mount Tam this morning. It is both objective and also partly in the eye of the beholder, made conscious through the eye of the individual imagination. We may see even the most humdrum thing, a plastic bag dipping and diving in the wind, for example, and, like the characters in the 1999 movie *American Beauty*, stop in awe at its inexpressible beauty dancing before us.

Beauty is one of the saving graces of being alive. As Anne Frank reminds us, it is always there for the looking, even in the ugliest of circumstances. If we keep faith with beauty, then we can keep faith with life. Beauty is worth being alive for. Our hunger and longing for it are intrinsic to being human. At beauty's root is the sheer delight, the awe, and the gratitude of experiencing the transcendent here on earth. "Transcendent," meaning not a vision of some other world, but the things of this world raised to their highest station through the quality of our looking. It is what Saint Augustine must have been thinking when he said, "I asked the earth, I asked the sea and the deeps, among the living animals, the things that creep. My question was the gaze I turned to others. Their answer was their beauty."

The natural world is the most immediate place we have to contemplate beauty. Even in a city, there is always a sky to look at and a tree to contemplate. It was the Romantic poets who first popularized nature as a quasi religion, with pilgrims plodding their way over hill and dale in the hopes of having what we today would call a peak experience. When you read lines like the following from Wordsworth's hand, it is hardly surprising that so many took up the call:

> Magnificent
> The morning was, a memorable pomp,
> More glorious than ever I had beheld.
> The sea was laughing at a distance; all
> The solid mountains were as bright as clouds,
> Grain-tinctured, drench'd in empyrean light;
> And in the meadows and the lower grounds,
> Was all the sweetness of a common dawn—
> Dews, vapours, and the melody of birds,
> And labourers going forth into the fields.
> Ah! Need I say, dear friend, that to the brim
> My heart was full? I made no vows, but vows
> Then were made for me: bond unknown to me
> Was given, that I should be—else sinning greatly—
> A dedicated spirit. On I walked
> In blessedness, which even yet remains. ❧

Wordsworth evokes here a natural religion, one whose church is the natural world and whose beauty can convey a sense of the spirit that lives and breathes in all things. His pantheism grew not from a preconceived ideal, as it may have done for his followers, but from his personal experiences in nature.

Today we live in a natural world vastly different from the one Wordsworth knew. In England, especially, there are very few wild and remote regions left, and the nature lover must content herself with well-worn paths and the company of many others out on a Sunday afternoon in search of a brief respite from a busy and preoccupied life. We have also secularized nature, squeezed it into a category of usefulness we now call "the environment." It has become a resource that needs to be preserved, managed, and utilized rather than wondered at.

Even so, it remains true that, for those with the eyes to see, all that is needed for nature to reassert itself is for us to lift our gaze, to stand and stare for a moment, to forget our concerns and open our hearts and minds to the larger world. And of course, America is still blessed with vast empty reaches of wilderness, deserts and forests, oceans and rivers that can return you to your proportionate place in the world and fill you with awe at the beauty of the planet we live on.

And what we have now that Wordsworth could never have dreamed of is the greatly expanded vision of the universe that science has made available to us. The natural world has expanded far beyond even our own planet. Through the medium of photography, science is giving us far more beautiful images than the current world of art seems to be presently capable of. You might even say that photography and science are replacing art in the higher purpose of reflecting our joy and wonder.

This is the argument of Jonathan Jones in his essay "Science Is More Beautiful Than Art," published in *The Guardian* in September 2012. Go to the website of the Hubble Space Telescope (hubblesite.org), he urges, and just feast your eyes on the wonder of the Eagle Nebula or the Whirlpool Galaxy. Visit the Hubble movie theater to take a tour of the cosmos, Jones says, and witness "the birth-throes and death-pangs of stars."

The physicist Richard Feynman has said that he would have arguments with an artist friend over the experience of beauty. "You can't improve on the sheer delight of beholding that yellow flower," his friend said. "I don't agree," said Feynman. "I see more than you see in that flower. I see the cells' inner structure and the processes by which it attracts insects to it, and I am filled with wonder and also curiosity by what I see. Can insects see color, I wonder? Does an aesthetic sense exist in lower life forms? I believe that science can only add to the mystery and beauty of the flower."

While it is true that the art of the last thirty or forty years has turned its back on beauty as a primary value and replaced it with the shock and awe of installations and performance art typified by such characters as Damien Hirst and Tracey Emin, that still leaves us with a few thousand years in which societies everywhere made art and buildings and objects whose primary function was to remind us of the transcendent dimension of being alive.

In his book *Religion for Atheists,* Alain de Botton proposes that museums be reorganized to educate us in the qualities that art can instruct us in. Instead of having the nineteenth-century gallery, for example, you would have rooms dedicated to courage, compassion, forgiveness, and so on. But this is a rational and reductionist view of the value of art and of religious art in particular. In his atheistic certainty, de Botton scoffs at any notion of the transcendent and reduces it to the merely ethical.

Art, and especially religious art, is not solely for our instruction, though it may also be that. Giotto's *Massacre of the Innocents,* Masaccio's shattering *Expulsion from Paradise,* Picasso's *Guernica,*

Munch's *The Scream,* not to mention all the representations of Christ on the cross, plunge us into the depths of human suffering and despair. They make us feel our common humanity and so, in their own way, transcend our narrowly personal preoccupations. Yet art's purpose for millennia has also been to lift us out of ourselves, out of our familiar world and sense of who we are toward the sublime. We do not have to be religious to be touched by the transcendent, to feel exalted by a Bach sonata, a Gothic cathedral, or a Fra Angelico fresco. A spiritual sensibility is integral to who we are as human beings, and the experience of it is not dependent on religious themes.

Some are sensitive to the beauty in art to an unusual degree. Stendhal syndrome is known to affect a number of tourists every year in Florence. The French author Stendhal was in 1817 so overwhelmed by the Renaissance masterpieces of the city that he could barely hold himself upright upon leaving the Basilica of Santa Croce. We can be fairly confident that it wasn't any ethical or moral lesson that caused the writer's reaction. Still today, staff at the local hospital commonly treat people for spontaneous tears, trembling, and fainting fits brought on by seeing Michelangelo's David or walking through the Uffizi Gallery. In one of Proust's novels, a character expires at the sight of a Vermeer. The German writer Goethe, a contemporary of Stendhal, was probably not thinking of such fervent reactions when he advised that "a man should hear a little music, read a little poetry and see a fine picture every day of his life, in order that worldly cares may not obliterate the sense of the beautiful which God has implanted in the human soul."

A little music, a fine picture, is more available to us now than at any time in history. You have only to go to the website of Khan Academy (khanacademy.org) to watch a free five-minute lecture on any one of hundreds of great works of art. The world's poetry is online in any number of sites, such as poetry.org.

The beautiful does not need to be a grand statement. In my teens I would spend hours in the tiny church of Saint Catherine's, a twelfth-century attachment to the old manor house in the quiet valley where I grew up outside Bath, in England. I would sit there alone, entombed in cool silence. Whitewash covered the plain walls of the interior. The only decoration was the sixteenth-century painted wooden pulpit and the little stained-glass window in the tower, showing the white dove of Saint John descending. The church's plain beauty would restore me to a post-rational, rather than pre-rational, sense of order and harmony. Later, I would come to realize that it was also the symmetry of its proportions that gave the little place its power. I would wonder at the peace that seemed to descend on me whenever I stayed in that little church alone and why that peace seemed to leave soon after I returned to the world beyond its gates. Such a simple brush with beauty, one that people everywhere, secular or religious, are familiar with.

Whether it be a little chapel like Saint Catherine's, a great cathedral like Chartres, or the Blue Mosque in Istanbul, it isn't difficult to come across a religious sanctuary that stops you in your tracks with the power of its beauty. Such places were designed to bring us to our knees in the admission of a force at work on us greater than our rational mind can appreciate or understand—a force consciously articulated by artists a few hundred years ago in what was still an age of religious faith.

But what of the beauty in a loaf of bread or a basket of apples? Of Fifth Avenue or even Macy's? Today we have a different conception of the sublime than the builders of the great cathedrals did. Ours is a secular vision, in which the humblest, most ordinary objects and scenes from everyday life have the capacity to shed an uncommon light on the world.

The most popular art in the West is that of the impressionists and post-impressionists. Gone are the religious motifs and subjects, replaced with landscapes and plays of light on people and buildings, as in Monet's *The Saint-Lazare Station* or his painting of the Boulevard des Capucines in Paris. The impressionists sought to convey the light, the radiance of a moment in time—a radiance that was dependent not on the subject of the painting, but on the capacity of the artist to see the beautiful in the fleeting moment. Stendhal called these "moments of beauty."

Already in the eighteenth century, the notion of the sublime and the beautiful had been largely liberated from a dependence on religious subjects and thinking. In an essay called "Against Sainte-Beuve," Proust imagines a young man of modest means looking around his humble home and feeling disgust at its ugliness. Proust takes him to the Louvre and into the eighteenth-century gallery, with its pictures by Chardin.

> And once he had been dazzled by this opulent depiction of what he had called mediocrity . . . I should say to him: Are you happy? Yet what have you seen here but a well-to-do bourgeoisie pointing out to her daughter the mistakes she has made in her needlework (*The Industrious Mother*), a woman carrying loaves of bread (*The Return from Market*), a kitchen interior where a live cat is walking over some oysters, while a dead ray-fish hangs on the wall, a sideboard already half cleared with knives left lying on the tablecloth (*The Buffet*). . . .
>
> If you now find all this beautiful to look at, it is because Chardin found it beautiful to paint. And he found it beautiful to paint because he found it beautiful to look at. You had already experienced, unconsciously, the pleasure that the spectacle of modest lives or of still-life affords, else it would not have arisen in your heart when Chardin came to summon it with his brilliant and imperative language.

> Your consciousness . . . had to wait until Chardin came to
> take it up inside of you and raise it to consciousness. Then
> you recognized it and savored it for the very first time. ൭

To open our eyes to the beauty of the world around us was for
Proust the great purpose of art. So it was for van Gogh, for
Matisse, for Renoir, for Bonnard, and for countless other artists
whose vision of the world proclaimed a secular, but not religious,
spirituality.

The American abstract painter Barnett Newman wrote in his
essay "The Sublime Is Now" (1948),

> We are reasserting man's natural desire for the exalted, for
> a concern with our relationship to the absolute emotions.
> We do not need the obsolete props of an outmoded and
> antiquated legend. . . . Instead of making *cathedrals* out of
> Christ, man, or "life," we are making them out of ourselves,
> out of our own feelings. The image we produce is the
> self-evident one of revelation, real and concrete, that can
> be understood by anyone who will look at it without the
> nostalgic glasses of history. ൭

To make cathedrals out of his own feelings could be a way of
describing the aim of another artist of Newman's time, Mark
Rothko. Barnett Newman's steel sculpture *Broken Obelisk* stands
in the middle of a pool at the entrance to the Rothko Chapel in
Houston as a memorial to the life and work of Martin Luther
King, Jr. The chapel, which opened in 1971, was built by the
art patron Dominique de Menil as a sacred place for people of
any religion or none. Her aim was to inspire people to action
through art and contemplation, to nurture reverence for the
highest aspirations of humanity.

Inside the windowless octagonal building, the eight walls are covered by fourteen of Rothko's monumental paintings, commissioned specifically for this setting. Tens of thousands of people visit the chapel annually to contemplate the paintings there in the cool silence. Rothko is best known for his radiant works of color, floating squares and rectangles, one above the other, in a space unbounded by a frame. But the paintings in the chapel are all variations on a purplish black, or blackish purple, with many uneven washes of pigment that create variations of tone in every inch. Whereas his color works keep the eye mainly on the surface, the Houston chapel paintings are invitations to step into a beyond. They have a spiritual intent without being religious. Their beauty bears no relation to conventional religious forms because they are not answering to a traditional society's understanding of reality. We don't have the same sense of hierarchies that we did even a hundred years ago, and most of us don't have a god. Rothko was not religious, but he created a beauty in the Houston chapel that draws you down into a silence and wonder that is at the heart of religious experience.

Many have mourned the passing of traditional forms and wonder if we are in a new age of crass individualism, where beauty has become an irrelevance. There have been plenty of complaining voices, not least among them Prince Charles, in response to what has been called the soullessness of postmodern art and architecture. And yes, it is true that the contemporary art market is dominated by works designed to shock rather than to elevate or illuminate. It is true that many Western cities are blighted with mid-twentieth-century blocks of glass and steel that bring a depressing anonymity to both living and work places. Even so, there are still good reasons to keep faith with the beauty being created in our public spaces. The twenty-first century is promising to be one of the most innovative periods for architecture ever, a period in which architects are stretching the boundaries of our feeling for the beautiful.

Frank Gehry, Rem Koolhaas, Norman Foster, Zaha Hadid, Santiago Calatrava, and many more artists are revolutionizing our understanding and feeling for the way public architecture can be both functional and beautiful at the same time, how it can serve to amaze, delight, inspire, and uplift even as the building's function is as apparently mundane as a train station or an airport. Monet, remember, painted railway stations as readily as he painted cathedrals. As many people visit Gehry's Guggenheim Museum in Bilbao, Spain, to gaze at the building itself as to look at the exhibits inside. Why? Because its dancing metal wave structure, sitting on the edge of a river, is beautiful in ways we have not contemplated before. It opens our vision to a new way of seeing and stretches our conception of what a building can look like.

Calatrava's Alamillo Bridge in Seville, Spain, is the delicate beauty that brought him worldwide recognition when it was completed in time for the Seville Expo in 1992. It looks like a swan about to take flight, and Calatrava's designs owe much to his studies of the human body and the natural world. He is also a sculptor and a painter, and claims that architecture combines all the arts into one. His first building in the United States was the Quadracci Pavilion for the Milwaukee Art Museum on the shore of Lake Michigan. It's another structure with a wing-like design, though a movable wing this time. For the people of Milwaukee, the Quadracci Pavilion has instilled a sense of civic pride and become a symbol for their city's aspirations.

Of all beautiful forms, the human face and body are, to human eyes at least, probably the most beautiful of all. The Greeks passed on their veneration of the human form in their marble sculptures of both men and women, while today beautiful faces gaze down at us from billboards in every city. Most major religions make use of the human face as an object of worship and devotion, from Christ Pantocrator to the Buddha. Symmetry is fundamental in our perception of beauty in a human face; but in the case of religious iconography, it's not just the symmetry, but also the expression of universal qualities like compassion and wisdom that the face mirrors back to us for our contemplation which make the images powerful.

If many top athletes are considered beautiful—to take only tennis, think Roger Federer, Andre Agassi, and Maria Sharapova—it is because they have been shown to have more symmetrical faces and forms than most of us. A symmetrical body, each side balanced evenly with the other, allows for greater athletic performance. But in an essay entitled "Federer as Religious Experience," the writer David Foster Wallace shows us that watching a top athlete in action can give us an experience of transcendent beauty far beyond the mere appreciation of symmetrical harmony:

> Beauty is not the goal of competitive sports, but high-level sports are a prime venue for the expression of human beauty. The relation is roughly that of courage to war.
>
> The human beauty we're talking about here is beauty of a particular type; it might be called kinetic beauty. Its power and appeal are universal. It has nothing to do with sex or cultural norms. What it seems to have to do with, really, is human beings' reconciliation with the fact of having a body. . . .
>
> A top athlete's beauty is next to impossible to describe directly. Or to evoke. Federer's forehand is a great liquid whip, his backhand a one-hander that he can drive flat, load with topspin, or slice—the slice with such snap that the ball turns shapes in the air and skids on the grass to maybe

ankle height. . . . His anticipation and court sense are otherworldly, and his footwork is the best in the game . . . . All this is true, and yet none of it really explains anything or evokes the experience of watching this man play. . . . You more have to come at the aesthetic stuff obliquely, to talk around it, or—as Aquinas did with his own ineffable subject—to try to define it in terms of what it is not.

One thing it is not is televisable. ৯

Wallace seems almost to be describing the experience of falling in love—not with Federer, but with the sheer radiance of his play, with the ineffable beauty of it. In love, as with the immersion in beauty, we are taken out of ourselves, raised up, made good. And it can happen anywhere, even while watching a game of tennis.

In one of his poems, Rumi speaks of going to a place beyond the dawn, to

A source of such sweetness that flows and is never less.
I have been shown a beauty there that would
confuse both worlds. ৯

Beyond the dawn means beyond our ordinary categories of light and dark, beautiful or ugly. It is a third quality, an eternal spring, confusing to the ordinary mind, beyond its distinctions. So how can we suggest that we have either seen it or not seen it? This beauty is not something we can point to; it is a condition to be lived and experienced, as Wallace experienced it watching Federer. This is why he says it was not "televisable." Wallace himself seems to disappear into the game. In that unified state, there is no separate observer to comment on it.

Rupert Spira, the spiritual teacher, has said, "When feeling is divested of the feeler and the felt, it shines as love; when seeing is divested of the seer and the seen, it shines as beauty." This is the beauty Rumi refers to when he says,

> When we have surrendered to that beauty,
> We shall be a mighty kindness, ✍

9

Keep Faith with
Kindness and Love

All the particles in the world
Are in love and looking for lovers.
Pieces of straw tremble
In the presence of amber.

RUMI

e shall be a mighty kindness," Rumi said. "My religion is kindness," the Dalai Lama says. "Practice random acts of kindness," the bumper sticker says. They are all speaking to a dimension of love that may seem small and commonplace, a cliché even, seeing as it has reached bumper-sticker status. We have heard kindness spoken of as a cliché so many times, but only because that cliché harbors a deep truth that can never be spoken enough. Kindness reaches deep down into the endless reaches of our humanity. It is where our love can begin and also end. Hafez says,

It happens all the time in heaven, and someday
it will begin to happen again on earth—that men
and women who are married, and men and men
who are lovers, and women and women who give
each other Light, will often get down on their knees,
and while so tenderly holding their lover's hand, with
tear-filled eyes, will sincerely say, "My dear, how can
I be more loving to you; my darling, my darling, how
can I be more kind?" ॐ

Hafez points to something far simpler and more immediate than many couples therapy or spiritual practices can offer. The heaven Hafez refers to is nowhere if not here, right here in the heart that is awake enough to respond with a spontaneous tenderness to the world as we find it. It is simple and immediate, but *only* when we can forget our self-importance and figuratively get down on our knees and ask the question of the moment we find ourselves in: how can I be more kind?

Once I was walking through the Sinai Desert with a Bedouin guide and two camels. My feet were sore, my legs were aching, the wind was whipping through me. Toward evening, Selman, my guide, hobbled the camels and lit a small fire. I clambered down some rocks to join him, my legs barely holding. I threw all the clothes I had on my back and lay down by the flames like a child, teeth chattering, vital force gone. Selman took his only blanket and covered me with it gently.

"Thank you, thank you," I mumbled.

"We are all brothers in the desert," he said, without affectation. I felt tears welling as I took in the simple kindness of ordinary human fellowship that survived in that desert still. No great emotion, the passing of a blanket and a cup of tea. Our shared circumstance not just the desert wind, but also the common lot of human frailty and kinship, the ceaseless wandering together, all of us, on the road from birth to death.

When we ourselves have known hardship and tribulation, as Selman certainly had, we are more likely to be able to notice and respond to the needs of others.

> Before you know kindness as the deepest thing inside,
> you must know sorrow as the other deepest thing. ❧

writes Naomi Shihab Nye in her poem "Kindness."

And while kindness more often than not means responding to some evident need—after all, action's great virtue is to transform kindness from an abstract quality into concrete form—it also refers to the way we breathe the air we breathe, the passage of kindness we leave as we walk through a room, the simple blessing our presence, anyone's presence, can bestow on the atmosphere of a moment. Ellen Bass puts it this way in her poem "Pray for Peace":

> Then pray to the bus driver who takes you to work.
> On the bus, pray for everyone riding that bus,
> for everyone riding buses all over the world ❧

I take her praying to mean a quality of beneficent attention, a recognition and embrace of others that can see further than their daily roles or worries or irritations. That kind of attention is ennobling; it is an expression of kindness as much as any direct action on behalf of another. "Attention is the rarest and purest form of generosity," Simone Weil said. Our attention is the one thing we have to offer at any given moment, and when we give our full attention to someone or something, it is an expression not only of kindness but also of love. It is the prayer whose god is whatever is before us.

> I don't exactly know what a prayer is,
> I do know how to pay attention . . . ๛

writes Mary Oliver in her poem "The Summer Day."

But let us shift from the language of poetry for a moment to the language of science, and from kindness into attachment theory. The one dimension of love that can be mapped by neuroscience is the one with its origins in our mammalian limbic brain. The first and most crucial love we can know is a mother's love—a flow of positive regard, attentiveness, affection, and loving concern. This is her limbic field, and if its resonance is felt by an infant in its positive form, he will gradually learn to look upon himself and others with those same qualities. Attachment theory has shown beyond doubt that an infant relies on the external resonance of his mother's limbic brain to feel a sense of security and belonging.

If not bathed in this resonance in his early years, he will be unable to internalize emotional balance later in life. He will be uncertain of his own identity and unable to form satisfying relationships with others. Without an internalized familiarity with limbic resonance, a child is unable to feel the internal world either of himself or of others. Lacking a stable center, he will look to external substitutes. The authors of *A General Theory of Love* tell us,

> Thwarted attachment and limbic disconnection thus encourage superficiality and narcissism. People who cannot see content must settle for appearances. They will cling to image with the desperation appropriate to those who lack an alternative. . . .
>
> Love is and always will be the best insurance against the despair for which street drugs are the obvious antidote.

Because mammals need relatedness for their neuro-physiology to coalesce correctly, most of what makes a socially functional human comes from connection—the shaping physiologic force of love . . . Recall that the brains of neglected children show neurons missing by the billions. ∽

It is the limbic brain that makes us so eager to form lasting attachments, be they with a romantic partner, children, groups, friends, or even the corporation we work for. Loyalty, concern, affection, and belonging are the limbic brain's natural inclinations. No one has given this kind of love a more eloquent voice than Gerald Stern in his poem "Waving Goodbye." His daughter is leaving home, and he hugs her

> as an animal would, pressing my forehead against her,
> walking in circles, moaning, touching her cheek,
> and turned my head after them as an animal would ∽

That is limbic resonance and attachment writ large. But can our limbic reality explain all the layers and subtleties of human love? Can it explain a spontaneous act of kindness, the offering of our attention to a stranger in need, or the world's love songs to God, the ecstasies of a Teresa of Avila or of a Kabir? Surely these kinds of love come from a dimension of our humanity that is likely to remain unmapped by neuroscience. We might say the same for the quiet love that permeates these lines of Robert Bly, in his poem "The Third Body":

> He sees her hands close around a book she hands to him.
> They obey a third body that they share in common.
> They have promised to love that body. ∽

We will surely never grasp in words and understanding the full extent of our reach as human beings. When the subject is love—which is indeed our farthest reach—I do believe that where science trails off into silence, imagination, with its language of myth, metaphor, and symbol, can lead us on into territory that we can intuit the truth of even as we may not fully understand it conceptually. This, I believe, is why Rumi says,

> Love has taken away all my practices
> And filled me with poetry. ✑

You will not find information or explanations in a poem, nor will you find them in a great painting or piece of music. What is found there is a deeper vein, one that transports us across different layers of meaning and provides a recognition of something through a felt sensibility, a shiver down the spine, rather than mere conceptual knowledge. After all, our feeling life reaches back a hundred million years, while cognition is a few hundred thousand years old at most.

This is why great works of literature and poetry about love can ring truer than our most sophisticated psychological theories, even after hundreds of years. This is why the love poetry of Rumi, Hafez, and Mirabai, the stories of Tristan and Isolde, Laila and Majnun, Abelard and Eloise, live on in their different cultures, from Western Europe to Persia and India, hundreds of years after they were first told. If Dante's *The Divine Comedy* and Shakespeare's plays are the foundational texts of Western literary tradition, it is because they and all these stories touch something eternal in us, beyond the personal and yet inclusive of it.

They are the fruits of Imagination—not *imagination*, a faculty by which an individual makes or thinks something up, but an eternal dimension of existence that is the realm of pure potentiality. It is a realm that gifted individuals have visited, or have been visited by, throughout time. This accounts for the both personal and impersonal tone of all genuinely creative activity, as well as genuine spiritual experience. It is why artists will often say the work doesn't belong to them as such, because it came through them. Think Mozart and his sonatas. The realm of the Imagination is the source of all creative endeavor, inspiration, and opening to a love that is not of this physical world alone.

In order to love, these great poems and stories say, you must have faith—faith not in a particular outcome (the love may well not turn out the way you would wish), but faith as the underlying and essential quality of a truly open mind. It is only in the territory of the heart, of love, that faith makes sense. In love, you cannot know what awaits you, which is why love is always a matter of keeping faith. You must step beyond the known and risk belonging, risk letting down the drawbridge of the ego's castle and stepping beyond yourself into another's world.

For all the delight it can bring, love is not easy. It is not easy because most of us are not easy. We throw up smokescreens; we duck and dive; we forget who we are behind the fanfare of our daily drama. In loving another, in loving ourselves, the field of loving presence must be open and spacious enough to welcome all comers—disappointment, hurt, misunderstanding, betrayal. These and the many other feelings that snap at our heels from time to time must be acknowledged and given their due place in the totality of who we are. But so too when we love another, must we know to keep faith with what is essential in them and also in us, even as it may seem to fade behind our own fog of confusion or in the storm of their emotions.

To keep faith with love is to keep faith with truth, to be willing to see and acknowledge one's own and another's blindness and shortcomings, and to place them in the fire of love, that the flames may burn even brighter. It is only a deep and loving acknowledgment, an acceptance of our obscurations, that can ever redeem them and include them in the integral wholeness that we are. And what is true for us holds true in our regard for others. Love challenges us to accept our beloved in his or her wholeness, which includes his or her imperfections.

How might we put this into practice? In my book *Twenty Poems to Bless Your Marriage,* I write that the old marriage vows, the ones in the Book of Common Prayer, have some answer to that, and not only for married couples:

> They speak of honoring and cherishing your beloved. When you honor someone, you hold them in deep regard. When you cherish them, you value them; your heart goes out to them. You want what is best for them, regardless of what it might mean for you. Your love is based on your wish for their highest good, and not on your own self-preservation. To cherish someone is to hold them in a loving regard; in a field of energy and attentiveness that nurtures. Anyone in a marriage or long-term relationship will be familiar with this field; though it will be tested frequently by events and temperaments as you journey together through the years.
>
> How does it feel to be in the warmth of a loving regard? Like a plant might feel as it turns toward the sun. We want to be close to them, touch them, make love with them maybe, or simply hold their hand. I would say the heart door springs open, and some of our self-concern dissolves like mist in the morning light. Then, when we love another deeply, we engage the soul; and the soul whose nature is relatedness, feels all things. The soul is the poetic and religious term for limbic resonance: we feel our partner's joy and also their pain; we feel the tension of their doubts and fears, the tenderness of their hopes and dreams. Not as

codependents who have merged their identities, but as two individuals who stand side by side in support of each other. A sustained loving is the work of an authentic individual; one who does not lose herself in the loving. We do not lose ourselves in the loving when we commit to awareness, rather than to the thoughts and feeling that pass through awareness. ॐ

To extend love and self-acceptance to ourselves, we may have only to look in the mirror, perhaps also get down on our knees, as Hafez suggested in the lines at the beginning of this chapter. To look in the mirror and, as Derek Walcott advises in his poem "Love After Love," to love again

> the stranger who was your self.
> Give wine. Give bread. Give back your heart
> to itself. ॐ

When we remember ourselves in this way, a communion of sorts can take place within us. Walcott reminds us that this love—this gladness at the sheer fact of belonging at last in your own skin—is not something new, but renewed. You were probably aware of it in your childhood, or in your teens, until it became obscured by the anxieties and preoccupations of the social self as it tried to make its way in the world. All the outpourings of romantic literature have been to the other, to the beloved in the form of someone else. Walcott reminds us that the beloved is also the one inside the cave of our own heart. Ultimately, this is the true sacred marriage, the union between our relative and transcendent dimensions of being.

Before such an inner marriage, there is usually a lifetime of remembering and forgetting. For moments at a time, for days at a time, we may know that the silent center of who we are is nothing but the love that made the world. It may not feel or sound as grand as this. It will likely feel ordinary, even nothing to speak of, because it is self-evident. But we will be in the center of ourselves, tender and open, and from there we shall feel in community with the world.

And then we forget. The world presses in, is *too much with us,* and a longing arises for something we have no name for, though some call it *God.* Most of us have known that longing and the feeling of absence it seems to emerge from. It is prior to religion, prior to philosophies of any kind. It is fundamental to the human experience. And this longing, perhaps more than anything else, points to what we already are, even as it may not feel like it. You cannot long for something you do not already know. The seventeenth-century French Catholic writer and philosopher Blaise Pascal, putting words in his God's mouth, said, "You would not seek me if you did not already possess me."

Once we have known this love that we already are, it leaves a mark that never entirely fades away. It is beyond time. It is this timeless love at our core that can find a mirror in the love of another. Then we can recognize that "Love's not time's fool," as Shakespeare puts it in his Sonnet 116. "Love does not alter when it alteration finds."

A deeper love that does not fade with time, one to which many couples who have lived a lifetime together can testify, is the love that Robert Bly speaks of in "The Third Body," excerpted earlier. It is the temple that Kahlil Gibran describes in *The Prophet,* a temple that is supported by two pillars standing side by side, upholding a sanctuary that is greater than either of them. When love travels deeper than emotional attachment, *while accepting the attachments as part of the whole,* it enters a region where two or more people are joined in the eternal.

Then a quietness of presence emerges, in which both individuals are witness to and aware of a greater life than their own personal preferences and needs. What Bly calls "the third body" will always be greater than the sum of its two parts. If we were Christian, we might call it "being joined in the Holy Spirit"—a phrase heavy with baggage, but beautiful nonetheless, and pointing to a dimension of existence that human beings of any religion or none have always recognized the world over. The Holy Spirit is the realm of the Third, which in Sufism is known as the realm of Imagination and in Celtic lore as the Holy Grail. It is the missing ingredient that miraculously brings meaning, purpose, peace, and union to the two opposing poles of our familiar dualistic experience. The old Russian sage George Ivanovitch Gurdjieff had a lovely name for it. He called it "the Holy Reconciling."

The quality of love that acts on a couple, or on friends, from the realm of the Third is more, not less, conscious than our ordinary eyes. Individuals are at the same time fully themselves and yet united, rather than fused; they are awake in a loving field that transcends either of them. That field is not from anywhere else, not spatially above or below, or only interior or exterior to them, but it is from a higher order of being that suffuses them and all things.

The popular figure of Cupid, on the other hand, makes lovers less conscious. Cupid is the familiar face of romantic love, with "its bounty and half-life of two years," as the poet Jack Gilbert puts it. The little figure with his bow and pouting lips is the shadow side of romance, when the light and energy of a connection beyond the ego take over your whole view of the other, making you blind to their humble humanity. Both parties fall prey to infatuation and are blinded by the unresolved dynamics of their unconscious material. More than once in my life I have been struck by Cupid's bow, and I have learned over time that trouble nearly always follows close on Cupid's heels.

Love, however, is more than an emotion that comes and goes. The kind of bond that is beyond time blurs the edges between the personal and the transpersonal. No one is the source of this love; it is its own source, which circles through each individual. It is the guiding spirit in a relationship, a creative principle somehow distinct from either partner and yet intrinsic to the relationship, circulating as the unity we know with our beloved. To allow it to flow, we need to keep one foot in the eternal dimension of the union and the other in the practical, everyday personal world of me and you. This is the foundational challenge, the koan, even, of becoming a full human being: to consciously bridge the worlds of matter and spirit without neglecting the one for the other.

This could pass for the description of a higher lovemaking. Sexual union can bridge the worlds. It is the royal road through which many of us come to taste the ecstasy in which self is forgotten and the world opens up to become a universe dark with the light of a million stars. Small wonder, then, that the mystics of all traditions have used the metaphor of a human relationship, and in particular sexual union, to describe the ecstasies of union with God. The love of one person for another becomes a microcosm of the love, the binding force, that makes and continually remakes the worlds. This is the poetic, imaginal truth of the world we live in.

The deepest faith one can have in one's love for another is that it can be an opening to this larger, universal love that is the foundational core of our own being and of all beings everywhere. But this is meaningless as a concept. It can only inhere as a lived experience; the experience is what we can have faith in—not a blind faith in one experience frozen in time, but a doubting faith that welcomes progressive insight and understanding over time and is corroborated by others. Often, even for mystics, the catalyst of another human being is required to make us fall out of ourselves into the dazzling dark beyond all names.

That kind of passing through the other into the vastness does not necessarily need to be sexual at all. Dante was catapulted onto his journey by the sight of Beatrice, a nine-year-old girl. John of the Cross was inspired by Teresa of Avila, Saint Francis by Saint Clare. Rumi was illuminated by Shams. Hafez started his spiritual life with a heart-opening vision of the inner beauty of a young girl he saw in the streets of Shiraz. These men and women saw through to the core of the human heart and beyond. See this, and you die. You die to the conventional self and enter a more real existence—an eternal, knowing, and loving field in which there is only one living and breathing aliveness encompassing all things.

You might think that such experiences are known only by rare individuals, such as a Dante or Hafez, but no. Countless people have had similar experiences that have not been recorded. Patrick Houck, however, is one person who wrote his experience into a poem. What happened to him took place in the most mundane of circumstances. Houck is a member of a writing group that I run. The class met a few hours after I had written the above paragraphs. I had mentioned my theme to no one. Patrick's offering that evening was a poem he had written about an experience he had had the week before. After he had read it, we were silent for several minutes. I can only say that I knew for a certainty that every word was true. This is the poem that Patrick read to us that night:

> 8 year old Julia is my neighbor,
> we met 3 weeks ago
> when she asked if she could pet my dog.
> Kneeling, she gently took Zoe's soft and furry ears

into her hands, like they were precious jewels.
She brought the entire world down with her,
in a pure and tender moment.
She stood, thanked me and walked away.
that day, I felt the
immensity of her heart.

today at my closed gate, I'm leaving for work,
my heart like a clenched fist.
Julia stands on the other side, ready for school,
looking right into me.
all snug in her quilted pink coat,
her clear eyes free of the future.

She holds me in her gaze
and I take the first breath of the day.
I grow nervous as the one who thinks he knows himself.
she continues to look into me,
A transparent sincerity.
And I, so vulnerable to this beauty and love
So afraid of losing control,
of being helpless before someone so young.
before anyone.
Yet the love softens that too.

From the inside out,
my whole body opening wide,
gentleness pouring over everything,
bringing down the inner scaffold,
Thought falling away, insignificant,
incapable of knowing such immensity.

then all the way down my heart is breaking, down into a vast,
infinite love
where we both are ageless, without concern, sacred.

I see reality shining fully . . . in Julia, in this moment, everywhere.
only what sees is not just me,
what's seeing is also looking from everywhere.
we are in the forever ancient.

She raises her hand, a greeting
and a goodbye.
I raise mine, she turns and walks off to school.

later, as I head down a new street,
looking at the freshness of things,
I am shaking.
Shaking with the certainty
that I have just known God. ✌

The mystical love union, in which there is no boundary
between your own awareness and the awareness that "rolls
through all things," as Wordsworth put it—for they are the
one and the same awareness or consciousness—is the aspiration of all mystics of any religion or none. It may come upon
us through the medium of another human being or in any
number of other ways. You may be in formal meditation, but
you may also be bending down to tie a shoelace and be struck
by that lightning.

Once I was standing before a fresco by Fra Angelico in a
monk's cell. It was in the Museo di San Marco in Florence. The
fresco depicted the Sermon on the Mount. The disciples were
gathered in contemplation around Jesus. He was sitting above

them on a stylized rock, washed in a soft yellow that glowed on the wall of the cell. Christ's right arm was raised, his forefinger pointing to heaven.

I stood there entranced—by the luminous tones, lavender and green, of the disciples' robes, the remarkable simplicity of the scene, but especially by the look on the faces of the disciples. They were filled with a rapture, a tangible sweetness of love, that was somehow of this world and not of it at the same time. Their expressions seemed to show a love for Jesus, the man, and also for something else that could never be put into words.

My legs began to tremble; my back turned cold. The thoughts in my mind ebbed away. Unable to take my eyes off those beautiful faces, I fell into a deep silence. My strength failed me, and I sank slowly to the floor. How long I sat there, lost in an endless vastness, I do not know. But when I finally rose to my feet, I knew that I had been filled with the love that makes the world.

10

Keep Faith
with the Human Spirit

It began in mystery and it will end in mystery,
but what a savage and beautiful
country lies in between.
DIANE ACKERMAN

Experiences like the one I knew in San Marco come and go, even as they leave a trace. I am one who remembers and then forgets, and I write this book in the hope that we may be inspired to remember together more often. Because for all the mystical experiences of love and awareness we may be graced with, it is difficult sometimes to experience the undivided reality of all things in a world that appears so fractured and broken, when we ourselves feel at times so fractured and broken. It can be all too easy to lose faith, not only in ourselves, but also in the human race, especially when we watch the news.

The twenty-four-hour news cycle pours images into our living rooms from around the world of one disaster, atrocity, and act of inhumanity after another. Corporate and individual greed seem to be more rampant than ever. Political corruption is endemic. Materialism is sweeping the globe. It looks bad, and yet believe it or not, the reality is that we have never had it so good. Just step back fifty, a hundred, five hundred, a thousand years, and more with the social psychologist Steven Pinker and you will see what I mean.

He takes this journey back in time for us in his 2011 book *The Better Angels of Our Nature.* The romance of the noble savage, first popularized by Rousseau in the eighteenth century ("Nothing," Rousseau declared, "can be more gentle than man in his primitive state"), fed the nostalgia of the Romantic movement of Rousseau's century and flowered again in the 1960s, when everything tribal and prior to the advent of the nation-state was commonly looked upon as some utopian ideal of a harmonious community.

In the century before Rousseau, the English philosopher Thomas Hobbes wrote, "In the state of nature the life of man is solitary, poor, nasty, brutish, and short." The evidence shows that Rousseau was wrong and Hobbes was right, Pinker tells us. Forensic archaeology reveals that 15 percent of prehistoric skeletons show signs of violent trauma. Ethnographic vital statistics of surviving non-state societies and pockets of anarchy show, on average, 524 war deaths per 100,000 people per year.

By comparison, Pinker continues, Germany in the twentieth century, wracked by two world wars, had 144 war deaths per 100,000 per year. Russia had 135. Japan had 27. The United States in the twentieth century had 5.7. In this twenty-first century, the whole world has a war-death rate of 0.3 per 100,000 people per year. In primitive societies 15 percent of people died violently; now 0.03 percent do. That means that violence is 1/500th of what it used to be in prehistoric times. Jump forward a couple of thousand years or more, and England's long history of court documentation tells us that in fourteenth-century Oxford there were 110 homicides per 100,000 people. In mid-twentieth-century London, there was just 1 per 100,000 people. The figures speak for themselves.

How easy it is to forget the hazards of living in an era prior to modern medicine and science. In 1856, Pinker tells us in his book, 12.8 percent of central Londoners died of cholera, before Dr. John Snow discovered that the disease was due to contaminated water, and the city expanded the sewer system and stopped dumping untreated waste in the River Thames. How easy to forget too that before 1945, there were two new wars in Europe every year for six hundred years! Some people complained that in 2012 the Nobel Peace Prize was awarded to the European Union, which has enjoyed sixty years of peace since it was first formed. Look back at the historical record, and these sixty years seem little short of a miracle. They are, in any event, unique in the history of that continent.

In the wake of the colonial havoc its individual countries left around the world, and for all its current dysfunction and struggles, the European Union has, for the last sixty years, been at the forefront of promulgating international justice, human rights, and the principles of democracy around the world, even as it has struggled to bring together dozens of cultures, each with its own rich history and language, into what is beginning to be a federation of peoples unique in the history of humanity. Its course is vulnerable to innumerable setbacks, even to foundering altogether. But even to have come this far is an achievement unique in history, one founded on a genuine desire for peace and unity across a continent that had never known either. Quite apart from the economic ties it is founded on, the European Union is a long and challenging experiment in cultural alliances, a blurring of the geographical borders between member states with the aspiration of gradually wearing away the foreignness and potential threat represented by the "other." Any initiative with that aspiration must have profound spiritual implications.

Even greater changes are happening in other parts of the world. In the last thirty years, more people have been pulled out of poverty in China alone, and in a shorter space of time, than ever before in human history. Much of the developing world is going through its own industrial and technological revolutions at a pace that makes nineteenth-century England's look positively sluggish.

The "other" used to represent anyone outside the immediate family. Then the tribe became the common identity. The circle eventually widened with the inception of the nation-state. The concept of the nation-state itself expanded when the birth of America was centered not on ethnicity or language, but on a Bill of Rights for all its citizens, wherever they may have come from. With a straight face, Walt Whitman was able to write this in his poem "America" in the mid-nineteenth century:

> Centre of equal daughters, equal sons,
> All, all alike endear'd, grown, ungrown, young or old,
> Strong, ample, fair, enduring, capable, rich,
> Perennial with the Earth, with Freedom, Law and Love. ✎

Those lines may seem hopelessly romantic and hardly descriptive of the reality we are living now, a hundred and sixty years later, but Whitman caught the aspirations of his time and pinned them to the page. The whole ideology of creating a heavenly city on the hill seems quaint today and hopelessly naïve in its estimation of human nature. Not only Communism, but also the philosopher Francis Fukayama's vision, laid out in his 1992 book *The End of History and the Last Man,* in which benign capitalism gradually turns the planet into a pleasure garden for all, has been discredited by events. Utopian ideologies in general are fading, as is the grip of religion, which has always offered the ultimate utopia, though usually on a deferred reward plan.

But that doesn't mean we would be any more sober and clear-eyed if we were to lean toward the other extreme and take a dystopian view of the state we are in. Things don't look so good on many fronts. Our political democracy has become an oligarchy that governs largely for the benefit of the richest 1 percent of the population. Now, as ever, populations are manipulated and used for the benefit of their rulers all over the globe. It has always been thus and probably always will be.

Yet none of our current ills can diminish the extraordinary achievements that began with the Enlightenment thinkers of the eighteenth century and their philosophy of secular humanism. The abolition of slavery; the right to vote for all colors and both sexes; the spread of literacy and education; human rights, animal rights, environmental protections—all these extraordinary accomplishments of the human spirit, instituted into law, surely suggest that for all its bumbling foolishness and rabid self-interest, humanity is still connected to something more than the drive to mere self-preservation and -aggrandizement. Humanity remains connected, surely, to its own indivisible essence and despite itself seeks, even if unconsciously, to give expression to the spiritual truths that sustain it.

More and more subsets of society have since claimed their voice and their rights in the last few decades. People of any sexual persuasion, people with disabilities, the old, the young—everyone in the developed world now speaks out from their own corner, expecting inclusion and the acknowledgment of their equal value, rather than the exclusion and inferiority that have been the fate of marginal groups since time immemorial.

The circle of life has expanded in the last fifty years or so to include a growing respect not only for animals and plant life, but also for the notion of the earth itself as a living organism. This is a truly astounding achievement, even though this point of view is still in its infancy. It suggests an expansion of awareness beyond the narrow confines of our own self-interest and tribal/religious identities, an expansion that can be appreciated all the more easily when one visits a country like Saudi Arabia, which still retains the values of a preindustrial, quasi-medieval society. Surely this shift is as much a collective spiritual development as a social and cultural one, but it's a development coming from the ground up rather than imposed from on high. Societal and environmental pressures have instigated a rethinking of behavior and attitudes, obliging us to become more inclusive and less inclined to place ourselves at the center of the universe.

Trade, technology, and easy access to international travel are widening the circle of humanity beyond individual states to the point where, along with our local reality, we can now imagine ourselves to be members of a regional and even a global community whose many parts are all mutually dependent on each other. Before the Internet and television, most of us would never have known of all the disasters that now flash onto our screens from around the world. Nor would we ever have been able to feel empathy for the people caught up in those crises. We would never have been able to donate money or send help to them, to express our solidarity with their suffering, not because they are in our tribe or even our nation, but because they are human as we are.

Technological innovation is in itself morally neutral. Like religion, it serves as an amplifier for all that is human, the light as well as the dark. But in the same way that improved living conditions can be the catalyst for spiritual, as well as simply material, development, so too can technology. We know that with the satisfaction of basic human needs—food, shelter, companionship—more energy is available for deeper and subtler concerns. One of the purposes of a monastery, in any tradition, was to provide for these needs in a time when they were not easily available, so that the monks or nuns would be able to devote their attention to more-spiritual interests. Education, formerly the exclusive preserve of the monastery, but long since a universal in the West, equally widened the outer and deepened the inner worlds to a degree inconceivable in less privileged times.

So the question is this: are all these developments an indication of the evolutionary movement of the human spirit toward a deeper alignment with spiritual values, toward a more just, equitable, and morally, as well as materially, wealthy society? This question was at the heart of much nineteenth-century thinking, which built upon the rational humanism of the previous century. There is no doubt that we are less trapped in the survival mechanisms of the reptilian brain than we were in earlier times, when violence and threats to one's survival were a normal and familiar experience. Not being threatened on a regular basis allows for higher brain functions to activate and express spontaneous acts of kindness, empathy, selflessness, generosity, and love.

But does that necessarily mean we are on some predetermined, evolutionary upward trajectory of consciousness, as some spiritual leaders suggest? I don't know. I don't know that there can be a plan at all in a world where everything is creating itself moment by moment out of all the myriad forces at play. It is true that a secular spirituality is spreading across Western culture—a spirituality generally free from dogma and institutions, and founded more on personal revelation and insight. It is also true that many of the spiritual teachers who have emerged in the West in the last thirty of forty years are reinvigorating the public discourse on what it means to be a human being. Eckhart Tolle, a spiritual teacher with a global reach, wrote a book called *A New Earth*. In it he envisions a new form of society, one more aligned with spiritual values, emerging from what he expects to be the eventual collapse of our present form of civilization system.

I have profound respect for Tolle's teachings and their contribution to the cultural conversation in general. But the fantasy of a new earth has been around for a very long time, and it doesn't seem to be coming anytime soon. If there is an intelligence at play in the way life unfolds, both in our personal and collective lives—and surely we can intuit that there is—why does it have to be an intelligence imposed from some higher plane with a preordained plan of where we're all heading?

All the moral and material progress that humanity has achieved is surely due to multiple and random causes, ranging from the effects of the printing press to clean water to the spread of knowledge through conquest and trade to freak weather conditions and to the technological advances that came from wars, not to mention the birth of agriculture and the geographical accidents of fate that Jared Diamond speaks to in his book *Guns, Germs, and Steel*. This, an ongoing, spontaneous interplay of causes and conditions, rather than some vast plan imposed from on high, from another dimension, is the more likely picture of how we have got to where we are today. Cause and effect, far from being a hierarchical, linear process, is multi-dimensional like the hologram that life itself is; with everything acting upon everything else from all directions at once, including the directions of the past, present, and future.

And as Diamond makes clear in his second book, *Collapse*, the whole human enterprise is always desperately fragile and can crumble at any moment—most currently from population explosion, climate change, and political discord, according to him. Nothing stirs hope and fear (and book sales) more than the prospect of imminent catastrophe followed by the birth of a new world. It's as if, like the citizens in Constantine P. Cavafy's poem "Waiting for the Barbarians" (who are waiting for the barbarians that never come), we need something dramatic to be on the verge of happening, because otherwise life would be so intolerably empty. Yet humanity has weathered countless collapses both local and global and is still here, and still as mulish as ever, to tell the tale.

Not that the human spirit has had nothing to do with all this progress; not that we didn't stumble into the light more often than not despite ourselves, or somehow aid the process by untold and uncountable acts of goodwill and selflessness. But I don't know that our essential humanity, or the unmanifest intelligence that is prior to all existence, is trying to draw us into taking part in some universal plan of ultimate enlightenment on Earth. I don't know that it's trying to do anything. It is surely nothing but love. And love loves whatever is, however it is.

Can we acknowledge that we don't know what this incredible complexity we call life is for? That it may well not be *for* anything at all, since *for* implies a future goal, whereas a true life can only reveal itself in this moment that is living us now? When we fall into *this* orbit, when we sit up, wake up, and know who we are in this living moment, then we begin naturally to trust the Mystery that all of this is, wonderfully, majestically, tragically, beautifully, configuring and reconfiguring itself from moment to moment, without need of answers or explanations.

A realization such as this can happen in meditation, on a walk in the woods, or while gazing into our lover's eyes. It can happen when, for no reason, we embrace our imperfections, trusting that they too are part of this Mystery. It can happen when we bow to the dark places too, or to the truth inherent in change. It can happen when we simply let go of the struggle one morning, when we wake up and find our faith restored in Beauty, in Love, in the spirit that lives and breathes in all things, the spirit that we are and that everything and everyone is. It happens when we bow in a deep embrace of life just as it is, however it is.

Easy to say, but we all know that it's not always so easy to fall down and kiss the ground, especially when it seems so dark outside. And yet in the heart of that darkness, in September 2001, just after the World Trade Center attacks, the zoologist Stephen Jay Gould managed to write these beautiful lines in the *New York Times:*

> The tragedy of human history lies in the enormous potential for destruction in rare acts of evil, not in the high frequency of evil people. Complex systems can only be built step by step, whereas destruction requires but an instant. Thus, in what I like to call the Great Asymmetry, every spectacular incident of evil will be balanced by 10,000 acts of kindness, too often unnoted and invisible as the "ordinary" efforts of a vast majority. . . .
>
> In human terms, ground zero is the focal point for a vast web of bustling goodness, channeling uncountable deeds of kindness from an entire planet—the acts that must be recorded to reaffirm the overwhelming weight of human decency. The rubble of ground zero stands mute, while a beehive of human activity churns within, and radiates outward, as everyone makes a selfless contribution, big or tiny according to means or skills, but each of equal worth. . . .
>
> Word spreads like a fire of goodness, and people stream in, bringing gifts from a pocketful of batteries to a $10,000 purchase of hard hats. ஒ

This fire of goodness is the visible expression of what stands always beyond all notions of right and wrong. And Gould kept faith with this, the human spirit, in spite of all that had just happened on his doorstep in downtown Manhattan. His words reflect a larger, knowing presence than the frightened conditioned self that is so easy to inhabit in the face of darkness—a presence that reflects a larger reality than the neurons firing in our brain, that points to a felt awareness of a dimension beyond the separate sense of self, one in which we are one body, one mind, with everything that lives and breathes. That presence that we are knows there is an inscrutable wisdom in the way it all works—not the wisdom of some Creator looking on bemusedly at his creation, but a wisdom and intelligence inherent in all creation itself, as it shows up moment by fleeting moment.

The more that each of us is committed to knowing and remembering this, our true and shared identity with all life, the more our fractured world can heal. To be committed to this in whichever way and action our life allows is to live an engaged spiritual life. It is to keep faith with the knowing that although there are no guarantees for the future, humanity is worth loving, worth working for and praying for, no matter what.

Bibliography

Ackerman, Diane. *A Natural History of the Senses*. New York: Vintage, 2011.

Alighieri, Dante. *The Divine Comedy*. Translated by Henry Wadsworth Longfellow. Hollywood, FL: Simon and Brown, 2013.

Bass, Ellen. *The Human Line*. Port Townsend, WA: Copper Canyon Press, 2007.

————. *Like a Beggar*. Port Townsend, WA: Copper Canyon Press, 2014.

Batchelor, Stephen. *Confession of a Buddhist Atheist*. New York: Spiegel and Grau, 2010.

Bly, Robert. *Eating the Honey of Words*. New York: Harper Collins, 1999.

Cavafy, C. P. *Complete Poems*. Translated by Daniel Mendolsohn. New York: Knopf, 2012.

Chariton of Valamo, Igumen, comp. *The Art of Prayer: An Orthodox Anthology*. Edited by Timothy Ware. Translated by E. Kadloubovsky and E. M. Palmer. London: Faber and Faber, 1966.

Dawkins, Richard. *The Selfish Gene*. New York: Oxford University Press, 2006.

de Botton, Alain. *Religion for Atheists*. New York: Vintage, 2012.

Diamond, Jared. *Collapse*, rev. ed. New York: Penguin, 2011.

————. *Guns, Germs, and Steel*. New York: W. W. Norton, 1999.

Gibran, Kahlil. *The Prophet*. Eastford, CT: Martino Fine Books, 2011.

Gilbert, Jack. *Collected Poems*. New York: Knopf, 2012.

Gladwell, Malcolm. *Blink*. New York: Back Bay Books, 2007.

Hafiz. *The Gift*. New York: Penguin Compass, 1999.

————. *I Heard God Laughing*. Reprint, New York: Penguin, 2006.

————. *The Subject Tonight Is Love: 60 Wild and Sweet Poems of Hafiz*. Translated by Daniel Ladinsky. Reprint, New York: Penguin Compass, 2003.

Housden, Maria. *Hannah's Gift*. New York: Bantam Books, 2003.

Jung, Carl. *The Red Book*. Edited and translated by Sonu Shamdasani. Translated by Mark Kyburz and John Peck. New York: W. W. Norton, 2009.

Kahneman, Daniel. *Thinking, Fast and Slow*. New York: Farrar, Strauss and Giroux, 2013.

Keats, John. *Selected Letters*. Reissue, London: Oxford University Press, 2009.

Kuhn, Thomas. *The Structure of Scientific Revolutions,* 4th ed. Chicago: University of Chicago Press, 2012.

Larkin, Philip. *Poems: Selected by Martin Amis*. London: Faber and Faber, 2011.

Lewis, Thomas, Fari Amini, and Richard Lannon. *A General Theory of Love*. Reprint, New York: Vintage, 2001.

Lippe, Toinette. *Caught in the Act*. New York: Tarcher, 2004.

Machado, Antonio. *Times Alone: Selected Poems of Antonio Machado*. Translated by Robert Bly. Middletown, CT: Wesleyan University Press, 1983.

Merton, Thomas. *Collected Poems of Thomas Merton*. New York: New Directions, 1977.

————. *The Way of Chuang Tzu*. New York: New Directions, 1965.

Newman, Barnett, and Jeremy Strick. *The Sublime is Now: Early Work of Barnett Newman*. New York: PaceWildenstein, 1994.

Nye, Naomi Shihab. *Fuel*. Rochester, NY: BOA Editions, 1998.

————. *Words Under the Words: Selected Poems*. Portland, OR: The Eighth Mountain Press, 1994.

Oliver, Mary. *New and Selected Poems*. Boston: Beacon Press, 1993.

Ovid. *Metamorphoses*. Translated by David Raeburn. Reprint, New York: Penguin Classics, 2004.

Palmer, Parker. *Let Your Life Speak*. Hoboken, NJ: John Wiley, 2000.

Parnia, Sam. *Erasing Death: The Science That Is Rewriting the Boundaries Between Life and Death*. San Francisco: Harper One, 2013.

Pinker, Steven. *The Better Angels of Our Nature*. Reprint, New York: Penguin, 2012.

Po, Li. *Bright Moon, White Clouds: Selected Poems of Li Po*. Translated by J.P. Seaton. Boston: Shambhala, 2012.

Proust, Marcel. *Against Sainte-Beuve and Other Essays.* New York: Penguin Classics, 1994.

Rand, Ayn. *Atlas Shrugged.* Reprint, New York: Plume, 2009.

Rilke, Rainer Maria. *In Praise of Mortality: Selections From Rainer Maria Rilke's Duino Elegies and Sonnets to Orpheus.* Translated by Anita Barrows and Joanna Macy. New York: Riverhead, 2005.

———. *Letters to a Young Poet.* Translated by Joan M. Burnham. Novato, CA: New World Library, 2000.

———. *Selected Poems of Rainer Maria Rilke.* Translated by Robert Bly. New York: Harper Row, 1981.

Roethke, Theodore. *The Collected Poems of Theodore Roethke.* New York: Anchor, 1974.

Rumi. *The Book of Love: Poems of Ecstasy and Longing.* San Francisco: HarperOne, 2003.

———. *The Essential Rumi.* Translated by Coleman Barks. Reprint, San Francisco: HarperOne, 2004.

Saint Theophan the Recluse. *The Path to Salvation: A Manual of Spiritual Transformation.* Translated by Seraphim Rose and Saint Herman of Alaska Brotherhood. Platina, CA: Saint Herman Press, 1997.

Shakespeare, William. *The Complete Works of Shakespeare,* 7th ed. Edited by David Bevington. London: Longman, 2013.

Shteyngart, Gary. *Super Sad True Love Story.* New York: Random House Trade Paperbacks, 2011.

Stern, Gerald. *This Time: New and Selected Poems.* New York: W. W. Norton, 1999.

Sweet, Victoria. *God's Hotel.* Reprint, New York: Riverhead, 2013.

Walcott, Derek. *Collected Poems: 1948-1984.* New York: Farrar Strauss and Giroux, 1987.

Wallace, David Foster. *Both Flesh and Not: Essays.* New York: Little Brown, 2012.

Whitman, Walt. *Leaves of Grass: The Original 1855 Edition.* Mineola, NY: Dover Publications, 2007.

Wordsworth, William. *The Collected Poems of William Wordsworth.* Hertfordshire, UK: Wordsworth Editions Limited, 1998.

———. *The Prelude,* rev. ed. New York: Penguin Classics, 1996.

Wright, James. *Above The River: The Complete Poems.* New York: Farrar, Strauss and Giroux, 1992.

Acknowledgments

My gratitude first to the wonderful peer community of which I feel privileged to be a part. Both the thinking and the feeling that have gone into this book have been stimulated and creatively questioned over the years by Lama Palden, Richard Miller, John Prendergast, John and Jennifer Welwood, Sherry Anderson, Miranda Macpherson, Roger Walsh, Francis Vaughan, Sylvia Timbers, and many more in this thriving spiritual/creative/innovative matrix the world knows as the Bay Area. I also thank those unusual individuals who, throughout my life, have deepened my understanding and experience of these subjects through their personal presence and insight, from Archbishop Anthony Bloom in the early '70s to Jacob Needleman, Ram Dass, and Neem Karoli Baba in the '80s, H. W. L. Poonja, Ramana Maharshi, and still others in the 2000s. My gratitude also extends to my writing students—two of whom, Patrick Houck and Susanne West, have generously given me permission to excerpt their work in this book. Finally, I could not have asked for a more caring and supportive editorial team than I have found at Sounds True—to all of you who have worked on this book in one way or another, I offer a deep bow.

About the Author

As of 2014, Roger Housden is the author of twenty-one books, including the best-selling *Ten Poems to Change Your Life* series; four travel books, including *Saved By Beauty: Adventures of an American Romantic in Iran;* and the ebook novella *Chasing Love and Transformation.* Tennis star Maria Sharapova called his book *Seven Sins for a Life Worth Living* "one of the most inspirational books I have ever read."

His work has been featured many times in *The Oprah Magazine,* the *New York Times,* and the *Los Angeles Times.*

He teaches writing classes both online and in the San Francisco Bay Area. He also leads writing groups on various themes, exploring everyday life as spiritual practice. He moved to the Bay Area from England in 1998. For information on his classes and workshops, please visit rogerhousden.com.

About Sounds True

Sounds True is a multimedia publisher whose mission is to inspire and support personal transformation and spiritual awakening. Founded in 1985 and located in Boulder, Colorado, we work with many of the leading spiritual teachers, thinkers, healers, and visionary artists of our time. We strive with every title to preserve the essential "living wisdom" of the author or artist. It is our goal to create products that not only provide information to a reader or listener, but that also embody the quality of a wisdom transmission.

For those seeking genuine transformation, Sounds True is your trusted partner. At SoundsTrue.com you will find a wealth of free resources to support your journey, including exclusive weekly audio interviews, free downloads, interactive learning tools, and other special savings on all our titles.

To learn more, please visit SoundsTrue.com/bonus/free_gifts or call us toll free at 800-333-9185.

SOUNDS TRUE
many voices, one journey